THE HOROSCOPE OF THE DUKE OF

BORN: 23rd June, 1894   TIME: 10 p.m. GMT   PLACE: White Lodge, Richmond Park, Surrey

The Duke of Windsor was born when the Sun was in the Water-sign CANCER and the Moon, the 'ruler' of his sunsign, was itself in another Water-sign—PISCES. This means he had an extremely sensitive, affectionate, intuitive and idealistic nature. The prominence of the Moon in his horoscope, in the part connected with 'personality' gave him the 'common touch' —the ability to mix easily, a keen sympathy and understanding of people, and a tremendous zest for life, and the joys of life.

The rebel in his nature is indicated by the fact that when he was born AQUARIUS—the sign of the individualist—was on the Eastern horizon of his horoscope, and Uranus, the planet linked with Aquarius, was the most powerfully placed one in the whole horoscope, (incidentally Uranus is linked with divorce). These signs account for his strong non-conformist attitude, his challenge to the Establishment. Aquarius is also the sign of the humanitarian, the reformer. The fact that Aquarius was so strong in his chart, and also because the Sun was at a powerful angle to both Uranus and Mars, gave him the willpower to hold out against both Ministerial and family pressure at the time of the abdication.

The chart also clearly shows someone who would be torn between his sense of duty to the family (in this case the family being the nation as well as kindred) and his affections and love of personal freedom.

Other details of his life-history clearly reflected in his horoscope are as follows:—

His Abdication is shown by the position and aspects of the planet JUPITER at the time of his birth. Jupiter was the 'ruler' of his 10th house—his 'career' house; Jupiter was in the arc of the horoscope opposite this house, and closely linked there with the planets Neptune and Pluto. This would mean the 'throwing off' of status.

The Duke's marriage to a commoner who was of different nationality was indicated by the fact that the sun (the ruler of his 'marriage' house) was placed in his 5th house (love, romance) and in powerful aspect to the Moon in Pisces (the people) and both sun and moon were in powerful aspect to Uranus in the 9th house (connections abroad). Interpreted, this means a marriage, made for love, with a woman of the people who was also a foreigner.

Had Edward chosen to remain on the throne he would have been a very popular monarch, but financially the country would have suffered. World War II would still have taken place and we should still have had the break-up of Empire which has occurred. This is shown in the horoscope by Mars (planet of War) at a powerful but unfavourable angle to the Sun in Edward's horoscope; quite apart from the indication of War during his reign, it would also mean loss of overseas possessions through war or other causes.

KATINA THEODOSSIOU

EDWARD VIII
THE MAN WE LOST

EDWARD VIII
THE MAN WE LOST

A Pictorial Study

ROBERT GRAY & JANE OLIVIER

Foreword by Alistair Cooke

COMPTON PRESS

First published in Great Britain, 1972
by The Compton Press Ltd.,
Compton Chamberlayne, Salisbury, Wiltshire
© 1972 The Compton Press Ltd., and Robert Gray
SBN 9001 9311 5

Designed by Humphrey Stone and printed at
The Compton Press Ltd.

Photo Credits:
The Camera Press, Central Press, C.O.I.
Conway Picture Library, Fox Photos Ltd., J. N. Hare,
Keystone Press Agency Ltd., National Magazines, Press Association,
Radio Times Hulton Library.

FOREWORD

Seeing that wistful face wizened in the later years, almost a Levine caricature of jet-set boredom, I could not help recalling the savage epitaph written by Westbrook Pegler, the American columnist, the weekend that Edward VIII quit the throne and his native land: "He will go from resort to resort getting more tanned and more tired".

It seemed insufferably cruel at the time, for he was still the golden boy among the monarchs of the globe, but it was no crueller than the actuality, the thirty-six year exile that lay ahead. The Governorship of the Bahamas was an intermediate poultice between the twilight grandeur of being almost the last King-Emperor and the long night of his banishment on the trans-Atlantic social tour: Cannes to Paris to New York to Palm Beach, back to the Waldorf, on to Paris, and back again.

For all the sycophancy of his new-found court among the gossip-column aristocracy of brokers, real estate barons and cosmetic manufacturers, he really had no place to go and he knew it. It was not that he had ever been a deeply serious man, much less an intellectual. He was most at home with army and navy types, racing peers and golf pros; and the genes of his grandfather, mobilising to resist the bourgeois stolidity of his father, fired him to go after wealthy playgirls, American jazz,

the midnight to dawn amusements of what came to be called "café society". But he also had a genuine curiosity about the lands he had to visit and the gorgeous range of human oddities who inhabited them. He may have had no enduring interest in elections, defence statistics, Arab kingdoms, or unemployment, but the statesmen, generals, sheiks and labour leaders were always on tap to surprise and instruct him. And his official duties, though routinely irksome, provided both a discipline and a curiosity shop that kept him lively and inquisitive. Once he forfeited them, he had to fall back on his mistress as mother, companion, protector, disciplinarian and sole beloved. That she was all these things to the end was the one salvation he rescued, and it must have been a consoling revenge against the gossips who circled like buzzards waiting through the years for the ultimate humiliation, which never came, of a broken marriage.

The obituaries were kind, often to the point of forgetfulness about the crux of the Abdication. Even the *New York Times*, the daily encyclopaedia of yesterday's dead, glossed over in its sixteen columns the three insuperable obstacles to the morganatic marriage which today's liberal press assumes would have easily solved everything. First was the fact that the Commonwealth prime ministers were unanimously against it. Second was the fact, which the Commons was well aware of, that the King had been insensitively close to German Embassy socialites. (The luck of having George VI on the throne was generally applauded not simply when the Second War started but within months of the Abdication, when Edward committed the appalling *gaffe* of visiting Hitler to inspect his "housing projects".)

But what rallied Parliament to Baldwin, before the public even spotted a storm signal, was the actual threat of a rising King's party, posed by a Churchill temporarily blind to the strength of the English Constitution. If that had happened, it might have soon heralded the end of the monarchy itself, for what enough sensible men saw at the time was the profound anarchy inherent in a parliament suddenly subdued by a Royalist rump.

For the ten days that shook and toppled his throne, he was the saddest and loneliest man in the Western world. His private emotional turmoil hid from him something that he came to learn later. But I believe he learned it for keeps, with the kind of guilty relief of a cured cancer patient; namely, that he had been not merely a lover defied but a constitutional issue of shattering importance. It may explain the persistence of that baffled, wistful expression, as of a playful child that once stepped on a land mine.

A.C.

"The boy will ruin himself"

Edward VIII was the most widely popular monarch ever to ascend the throne. There was no disrespect for his father implied in the enthusiasm for the new king. George V's solid, pedestrian virtues and his unbending dedication to the traditional concept of kingly duty had won first the respect, and finally the affection, of his subjects. But he had not greatly troubled the placid depths of their devotion with glamour or excitement, and it was precisely these elements that his son now promised to provide. George V had personified a Victorianism that had long become extinct outside the bounds of his court, but Edward VIII was in the van of the new age. "I was, after all, the first king of the twentieth century who had not spent at least half his life under the strict authority of Queen Victoria."

Nothing appeared more fortunate than this dispensation. Impatient of convention, eager for experience, ready with sympathy, he also possessed a priceless gift, prospectively more effective in securing the love of his people than any of the institutional apparatus with which George V had sheltered his dignity. This was an ease, directness, and charm of manner which enabled him, even in the most casual encounter, to communicate his essential humanity to all sorts and conditions of men. All sorts and conditions of women, too, for Providence,

or, as Queen Mary preferred to think, Family, had included in the bounty it bestowed on King Edward a boyishly attractive appearance, the appeal of which was in no way diminished by an occasional and fleeting intrusion of melancholy. If to Lady Diana Cooper, watching him catch jellyfish in the summer of 1936, he appeared like a child of eight, there were other women more continuously sensible of his real age, forty-two.

Altogether it was no wonder the omens were fair: Prince Charming had entered his kingdom. As he hastened to inform his subjects, in the first broadcast which he made after his accession: "I am better known to you as Prince of Wales—as a man who, during the War and since, has had the opportunity of getting to know the people of nearly every country of the world, under all conditions and circumstances. And, although I now speak to you as King, I am still that same man who has had that experience and whose constant effort it will be to continue to promote the well-being of his fellow men . . . . ."

Thirty-six years later the three mile queue for his lying-in-state at St. George's Chapel, Windsor, showed that he continued to cast his spell. Could George V have suddenly arisen from his grave in the Chapel to witness the scene, he must have

That extraordinary magic . . . . he was a spell-binder.

rejoiced (though, to be sure, a likewise risen Queen Mary would speedily have disabused him) at a spectacle which provided every indication of a long and triumphant reign. He might have remembered the prediction he had made so many years before—"After I am dead the boy will ruin himself in twelve months"—and returned to the shades with relief, perhaps not untinged with resentment, that the boy's charm had after all enabled him to disprove that gloomy foreboding.

But of course the panegyrics trumpeted at his accession and the affectionate tributes elicited by his death were separated not by a glorious reign but by years of exile. The first anniversary of his accession found him an ex-king, wrangling with his brother and successor about the financial arrangements for his new role. He always insisted that he never regretted the decisions which he took in 1936, and that, faced a second time with the same choice, he would again surrender his throne to marry Mrs Simpson. There was never the least cause to doubt that he was telling the truth: even his expectations, pitched dangerously high, were not disappointed by his marriage. "Evidently he is still passionately in love", an observer reported in 1949.

While acknowledging this, however, it is difficult when recalling his career to avoid a sense of waste or to share his stoicism about his destiny. Was it indeed his highest potential that he fulfilled in making his choice? Was it necessary to separate himself from a country which expected so much from him and to exchange the crown of a king and an emperor for the ineffectual anonymity of the unattached exile? Was it really unavoidable that the promise of his youth should evaporate in trivial disputes over his wife's title, or that his proven concern about social conditions should finally be dissipated in the narcissistic and sterile inanities of international high society?

Every man will answer such questions according to his own

values. Edward himself stressed that he was not faced with a conflict between private happiness and public duty so much as with an awareness that he could never do justice to his position without Mrs Simpson. "You must believe me when I tell you", he told the nation in his abdication broadcast, "that I have found it impossible to carry the heavy burden of responsibility and duty as king, as I would wish to do, without the help and support of the woman I love". Many people did believe him, but the vast majority also accepted the Government's view that Mrs Simpson could not be queen. The origins of this attitude were complex and included a number of ingredients, such as anti-American snobbery, most unflattering to our national character. But the main issue at least was always clear: Mrs Simpson was divorced.

That this was regarded as an insurmountable obstacle puzzles, even outrages, another generation today, and renders the abdication crisis inexplicable to some except in terms of doctrinaire views of the class struggle. The permissive society rarely seems to feel obliged to extend the blessings of its tolerance to the moral systems of its predecessors. Rather, being itself increasingly inclined to celebrate its emancipation from those stuffy old values within the divorce courts, it is naturally censorious that the king should have had to sacrifice his throne just because his prospective consort had "two husbands living" (to see the matter with Queen Mary's unblinkered gaze). Some latter-day enthusiasts for Edward's cause talk almost as though such a choice was an index of his modernity, and his determination to carry it through a sign, unhappily extinguished, that the monarchy was ahead of the hypocritical moral standards of the age. Certainly it seems strange that a society which purported to subscribe to an ethic asserting the primacy of individual feeling should forthwith have booted out its figurehead simply for acting according to just such a code.

In reaction to this moral schizophrenia there has always been a tendency to see Edward as a martyr. Because the principles which forced his departure have seemed false to some, trivial to others, the suspicion has arisen that there were other forces at work. In particular it has been suggested that the 1930's establishment saw the new king as a dangerously radical figure, liable to threaten with his popularity its determination to maintain the *status quo* by means of reactionary social policies. A Tory-dominated government therefore seized on the golden opportunity, presented by the king's desire to marry Mrs Simpson, to remove the goading thorn. In this version, the years of exile that followed the abdication appear as the vicious revenge taken by the ruling class on the figure who had once menaced its sway.

Thus, ironically enough when certain of his views are remembered, Edward has gained the appeal of a victim, even in some left-wing circles. The honour and ceremony accorded him at his death were just further confirmation of the villainy of the Establishment. Speaking on 3 June 1972, Mr Ian Mikardo M.P. allowed his outrage to carry him still further. "In a generation from now, when we have quietly got rid of the monarchy . . . people will see the events of this week as the beginning of the end of the court and all the mumbo-jumbo that goes with it . . . When he was alive Edward Windsor was savaged and his wife contemned by the Court, the Established Church and the Government. Now, with sickening hypocrisy, they are falling over themselves to show to the corpse the charity they denied to the man . . . It is a sick joke. It is the habit of primitives to venerate in death what they have despised or ignored in life."

With his grandmother, Queen Alexandra, and a bevy of young Royals at Mar Lodge in Scotland. The Prince is second from the right.

Prince Edward at the age of ten. At this time King Edward VII was on the throne.

In childhood he was barred from the crowds.

The midshipman Prince and the senior naval officer.
In his early youth the Prince was seldom allowed
to mix with companions of his own age.

This picture of Edward the Martyr can be varnished with just enough facts to cover the gaping gaps in the canvas. There *were* well-established groups whose antagonism the king had aroused. Just possibly the Government *might* have stood a chance of saving Edward if it had recklessly risked its neck. But the realities of power do not encourage such chivalrous gestures, nor indeed (as we shall see) had the course of Edward's reign provided Ministers with any incentives to chivalry. The truth of the abdication remains far simpler, far more obvious, but no less interesting than the ingenuities of opposing theory: Edward himself both precipitated the crisis by his inflexible determination to marry and exacerbated it by his wilful refusal to compromise. The abdication was an act of self immolation performed in the cause of love, not an artificial contrivance manufactured in the cause of reaction. For the marriage which the king proposed to contract completely undermined his vaunted popularity. The reason, though few at the time would have put the matter so pompously, is that it conflicted with the very *raison d'être* of constitutional monarchy.

It is pointless to apply the presently lax standards of private morality to the behaviour of a constitutional monarch, because to do so must shake the foundations of his position. There is no need to rehearse at length the arguments for monarchy; they are set forth in Bagehot's *English Constitution* with a brilliance and a force all the more compelling because the writer acknowledges the dangers inherent in the institution as well as the benefits to be derived therefrom. But today, when there is daily increasing evidence that the bonds holding society together and binding it to government are becoming dangerously weak, the value of monarchy should more than ever be obvious. The Crown provides a neutral apex to the pyramid of society, a focal point for the loyalties of the whole nation. By doing so it maintains the notion of Britain as a single, unified society, however much sections of the country may be alienated by the policies of a particular government. And, if the feelings for the monarch are emotional rather than rational, why complain at that?

Granted that the Crown fulfils such a purpose, the more loyalty it can win, the better. Long ago the idea of divine right proved a powerful attractive force, but in the seventeenth century the decapitation of Charles I and the flight of James II suggested some infirmity of purpose in the divine will. The accompanying decline in the power of the Crown to compel spontaneous devotion necessitated the discovery of new loyalty-gathering techniques. The quality of the Hanoverians determined the most successful device. Instead of grovelling in terror before the anointed of the Lord, the people were first allowed, then encouraged, to discover how ordinary, how like themselves was their King. And so for rule by right was substituted affection by association. The fact that memories of divine right and supreme power still echoed faintly in the public conception of the sovereign only served to enhance the effect of the new image. Moreover, of all the associative links between Crown and subject, none evoked—or evokes—the required response so powerfully as that of the family life of royalty. As Bagehot wrote, "It brings down the pride of Sovereignty to the level of petty life. No feeling could be more childish than the enthusiasm of the English at the marriage of the Prince of Wales. They treated as a great political event, what, looked at as a matter of pure business, was very small indeed. But no feeling could be more like common human nature as it is, and as it is likely to be. The women—one half of the human race at least—care fifty times more for a marriage than a ministry. All but a few cynics like to see a pretty novel

Knight of the Order of the Garter.

touching for a moment the dry scenes of the grave world. A princely marriage is the brilliant edition of a universal fact, and, as such, it rivets mankind."

Thus the question of a prince's marriage cannot be dismissed as an irrelevant private matter, entirely separate from the prestige conveyed by his public office. The Royal Marriages Act of 1772, which provided that princes of the blood could not marry without the King's consent, specifically recognised the matter as an affair of state. Equally, by using the threat of resignation, a government can veto the marriage of the King himself. This, Baldwin told Edward, "was part of the price which the King had to pay. His wife becomes Queen; the Queen becomes the queen of the country; and therefore in the choice of queen the voice of the people must be heard." If the reputation of the monarch matters, then so does the propriety, or at least the appearance of propriety, in his family life: only republicans can logically be indifferent.

To condemn this insistent prudery about the monarch's behaviour as another instance of English hypocrisy makes no odds: the prudery remains. Indeed it appears that the English have required little more from their sovereign than a sense of duty, domestic virtue and longevity. George III went mad, but did not forfeit his popular reputation; Victoria became remote and ended by increasing hers; George V remained pedestrian and his reign culminated in a remarkable outpouring of public affection at the Jubilee. These monarchs could not be said to have challenged their subjects' imaginations, but still less could they be accused of challenging their morality. They were all earnest practitioners of what Byron stigmatised as "household abstinence". Admittedly Edward VII's rather more flexible approach to the pleasures of the hearth did not ruin his reputation; in fact enabled him to appeal as a stylish roué. But

From the Prince's own album.
LEFT Corporal in 1914.
RIGHT Ski-ing in Norway, aged 19.
FAR RIGHT In the Navy, 1913.

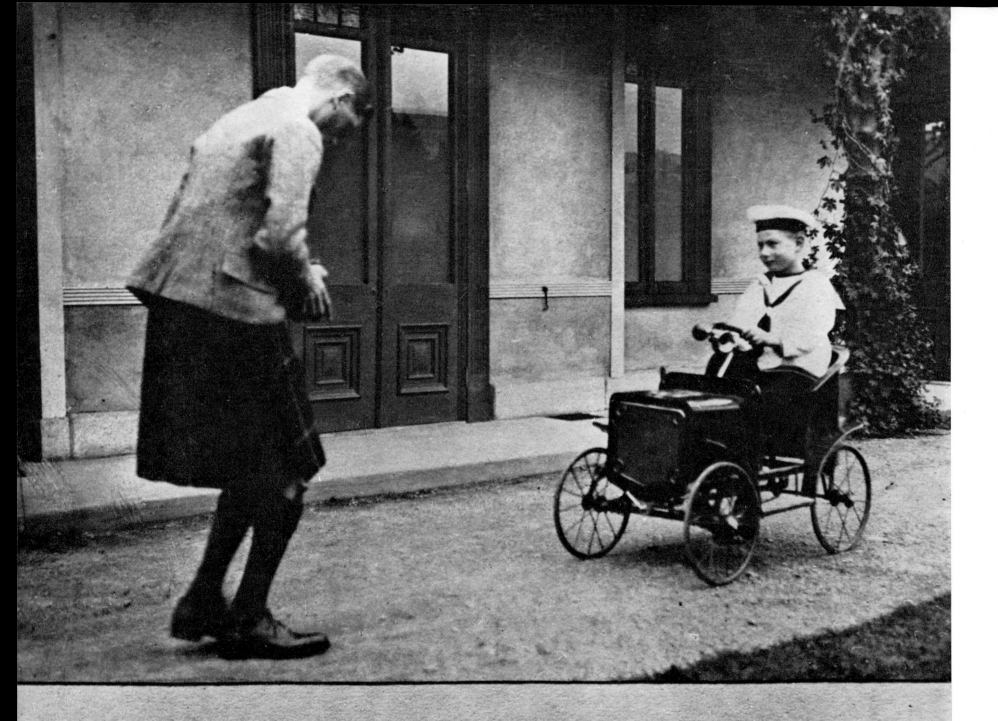

Self photographing John.

he was perhaps fortunate that he was almost sixty by the time he came to the throne. Probably a king's reputation could not have withstood scandals like the Mordaunt divorce case or the Tranby Croft gambling affair: even as Prince of Wales he was publicly hissed. Today, for all the riot of tolerance abroad, can one really imagine what a liaison between Prince Charles and a married woman would escape censure? No wonder that in 1936 King Edward's great popularity could not overcome the hostility aroused by his determination to marry Mrs Simpson.

If there had been division in the country on the matter would not the Opposition have jumped at the chance of exploiting it? Instead, the Labour Party, which had reverently acknowledged George V's reluctant decision that they need not wear knee breeches as remarkable evidence of his constitutional rectitude, now united behind Baldwin as though Edward VIII was bent on overthrowing parliamentary democracy. Its non-conformist conscience was outraged and the party's leader, Clement Attlee, supported the Government throughout the abdication crisis. Walter Citrine, General Secretary of the T.U.C., hearing the gossip about Mrs Simpson on a visit to America, managed "a sense of personal humiliation at the scurrilous allusions to the king's alleged carryings-on with a divorced woman". This "personal humiliation" bred the fear, conveyed to Baldwin, that the king "might marry her before the coronation and think he can get away with it". Not, Citrine was determined, if the Labour Movement could prevent it. The same point was made by J. H. Thomas, who had begun life as an engine-cleaner and, rising through the Trade Union movement, had become a Cabinet Minister and friend of George V. He told Harold Nicolson, "and now 'ere we 'ave this obstinate little man with 'is Mrs Simpson. Hit won't do,

'Arold, I tell you that straight. I know the people of this country. I *know* them. They 'ate having no family life at court". The unkindest cut of all came from South Wales which the King had visited in November 1936. On that occasion his obviously genuine concern at the conditions he found had been reflected in his famous protestation "Something must be done". The miners had appeared to warm to his sympathy but when Hugh Dalton visited the same area three weeks later he found that the non-conformist spirit had triumphed again. Local trade unionists "were unanimously and most emphatically against the marriage, morganatically or not. Many strong words, even some jeering words, were spoken against the King".

No less strong were some of the words used at the other end of the social and political spectrum. "The King", one Conservative M.P. felt, "has behaved like a petulant lunatic, and there is nothing to be done, except save him from himself. He must go . . ." Many other Conservatives were more saddened by the King's decision than so smugly censorious, but there were never more than about forty members prepared actively to support the King. Edward felt that he might rally support if permitted to broadcast during the crisis, but he was overestimating his influence on his subjects. "I do not find people angry with Mrs Simpson", wrote Harold Nicolson in his diary on 3 December 1936, "but I do find a deep and enraged fury against the King himself. In eight months he has destroyed the great structure of popularity which he had raised". And he noted that at a meeting in Islington only some ten out of four hundred people were prepared to join in the singing of God Save the King.

The so-called King's Party was in reality a heterogeneous scattering of ambition, discontent, die-hard monarchical

LEFT With younger brother Prince John who died in 1919. Another picture from the Prince's album.

sentiment and extravagant eccentricity. There were the Beaverbrook and Rothermere presses; there were Oswald Mosley and his Fascists, Harry Pollitt and the Communists; there were a few Conservative M.P.s and one or two Socialists; and there was Lady Houston who was convinced that Baldwin was acting on instructions from Moscow. She wrote to Queen Mary generously promising to pay all expenses if the Queen would go to Cannes and bring back Mrs Simpson to stay in Marlborough House.

But generally the British were enjoying "one of their periodic fits of morality" too much to share Lady Houston's concern. "We all share the Archbishop's regret that Edward VIII insists on marrying the woman with whom he happened to fall in love", a correspondent unburdened herself to readers of the *Sunday Referee*. And from America an Englishman wrote to the *Times* expressing his disgust at the joyously uninhibited salacity with which the American press were treating the affair ("King's Moll Reno'd in Wolsey's Home Town" ran one heading) and concluded with a suggested remedy: "nothing would please me more than to hear that Edward VIII had abdicated his right in favour of the heir presumptive . . . in my view it would be well to have the change take place while it is still a matter of individuals, and before the disquiet has progressed to the point of calling into question the institution of monarchy itself."

The attempt to indict the Government, or, even more amorphously, the Establishment, as the villain of the abdication drama therefore founders on the evidence of public opinion. Yet the charge still lingers, and, should the count of creating the crisis fail, the prosecution attacks the duplicity of the Government in handling it. In particular Stanley Baldwin, the Prime Minister, is accused of deliberately edging the King off the throne while outwardly extending the hand of friendship.

That the ex-King himself came to believe this is suggested by his memoirs which display a bitter animus against Baldwin. The Minister's efforts to warn of public hostility to the marriage evoke the contemptuous jibe that "He might have been the Gallup Poll incarnate". Even the Prime Minister's car does not escape Edward's derision. "I watched him wriggle into the same little undersized black box in which he had made his first descent on the Fort. As the box with its portly occupant shot away into the dark, it began to take on the guise of a sinister and purposeful little black beetle".

The case against Baldwin resolves itself into two main allegations. Both relate to acts of omission rather than commission and neither can be sustained with any compelling force. It is said, first, that his failure to confront the King at an earlier stage with the perilous consequences of the marriage, together with his passivity throughout the crisis, prevented Edward from adequately appreciating the stark alternatives and allowed him to nurse false hopes that he could marry Mrs Simpson without forfeiting the throne.

Baldwin certainly acted slowly. Perhaps he found it hard to believe that the King would actually make Mrs Simpson his wife. He must have acknowledged the possibility however, especially after meeting Mrs Simpson at a dinner party the King gave in the summer of 1936. "I own it surprised me to see Mrs Simpson at one end of the table and Lady Cunard at the other." Also, there is evidence that Mr Simpson's belief that the King would marry his wife had been reported to the Prime Minister early that year. Anyway, although throughout the summer and autumn gossip and speculation were rife in the foreign press and London society, it was not until 20 October that Baldwin brought himself to broach the subject with Edward. Then his purpose was merely to suggest that the

The Prince served in the army throughout World War I.
He waged a personal battle against his father who tried
to keep him out of the front line.

King should use his influence to prevent Mrs Simpson divorcing her husband, in this way scotching all rumour that he would marry her himself. Edward's firm refusal must have removed all doubts from Baldwin's mind. Still, though, he avoided pressing the King. It was Edward who forced the pace. On 13 November his private secretary ventured to write warning him that the silence which the British Press had observed would not be long maintained, and that, since there was small support for the King in the House of Commons, the resignation of the Government on the issue would be disastrous for the Crown. "If your Majesty will permit me to say so, there is only one step which holds out any prospect of avoiding this dangerous situation, and that is for Mrs Simpson to go abroad *without further delay*—and I would *beg* your Majesty to give this proposal your earnest consideration before the position has become irretrievable." The letter was couched in respectful tones but to the King it was a flung-down gauntlet. "I was obviously in love. They had struck at the very roots of my pride. Only the most faint-hearted would have remained unaroused by such a challenge." Summoning Baldwin to Buckingham Palace on 16 November, he made his position absolutely clear. " 'I intend to marry Mrs Simpson as soon as she is free to marry,' I said. If I could marry her as King well and good; I would be happy and in consequence perhaps be a better King. But if on the other hand the Government opposed the marriage, as the Prime Minister had given me reason to believe it would, *then I was prepared to go*". Although the spectre of abdication had already been hovering between the King and his Prime Minister, it was Edward not Baldwin who first openly acknowledged its presence.

This fact at once justifies criticism of Baldwin's hesitation and removes its sting. Clearly Edward had not been deceived

In 1919 the Prince of Wales was appointed Colonel in Chief of the Royal Scots Fusiliers.

Invariably he was the focus of attention. At a House of
Commons reception he meets the crew of the American
Airship N.C.4 which in May 1919 had just flown the Atlantic.

by Baldwin's delay into a false view of his position. He knew the stakes for which he was playing and he knew that he might not win. Lord Monckton, Edward's most intimate advisor over the abdication, saw the reason the apparent royal innocence. "He realised that if anyone in his service sufficiently clearly appreciated what he wanted to do, his plans would probably be frustrated."

The second allegation against Baldwin concerns the manner in which he explored the compromise solution that the King should marry Mrs Simpson morganatically. Such a device would have made Mrs Simpson the King's wife without her becoming queen. In view of the importance Edward later attached to the question of his wife's title, this solution could not have greatly appealed to him. For as *The Times* summed up the idea: "The Constitution is to be amended in order that she may carry into solitary prominence the brand of unfitness for the Queen's throne". But Edward was getting desperate: "I've got to do something", he said. The proposal was submitted to the Dominions and the charge against Baldwin was that by allowing this he was putting Edward into a vulnerable position. It is certainly true that the Dominions' rejection of the idea was a crucial blow to Edward, but the wound was self-inflicted. For when Edward first raised the question with the Prime Minister, Baldwin had clearly warned of the consequences that formal consideration of the idea would imply. Amongst these was consultation with the Dominion Prime Ministers. "Do you really want that, Sir?" Edward persisted; once again it was he who had forced the pace.

Some odd remarks made by Baldwin have also aroused the suspicion of Edward's protagonists. At the accession council he had mumbled his doubts that Edward would "stay the course" and he considered that "the Yorks would do it very well".

Again, on 8 December he confessed himself "frightened" that the King would change his mind about the decision to abdicate. Yet one need not find anything sinister in these comments. By 8 December the King had so far committed himself that he could not retract (in fact he had no intention of doing so) without irretrievable loss of face. As to the first remarks, they reflected shrewd judgement of the King's character rather than a ruthless determination to oust him. Certainly the fulfilment of his prophecy brought no pleasure. "It is totally unfair and untrue to say that Baldwin had stagemanaged the whole thing to get rid of the King", the Duke of York's Private Secretary considered. "A sentimental man, he was just as upset as everyone else. He hated every minute of it."

At the time Edward himself acknowledged the scrupulous fairness of Baldwin's dealing. Immediately on reaching France, after the abdication, he telegraphed Mrs. Baldwin: "Sincere thanks for your kind letter so much appreciated yours and Mr. Baldwin's great understanding at this difficult time. Edward." "Mr Baldwin", he said, "was the only man who said any kind word to me about the future or wished me luck". Already by the Christmas of 1937, however, Baldwin had become aware of a certain *froideur* from his former master, nor was he in doubt about its origin. "I have sent a Christmas card to the Duke of Windsor: I don't want our old friendship to die on my hands. Of course she will look over his shoulder and say: 'that old b——?' (or whatever may be the Baltimore equivalent!) 'pitch it in the fire'."

No, Mr Baldwin will not fit the role of Machiavellian manipulator, not in this story at least. Wherever one seeks them the search for scapegoats eventually founders on the essential fact of the abdication: Edward's unshakeable resolve to marry Mrs Simpson, whatever the consequences. From 1934 on his mind had closed like a steel trap on this decision and there was no force strong enough to prise it open. That tremendous battery which beat against him in the last month of 1936—his subjects' clamour, his cabinet's urging, his friends' repeated warnings, his brothers' dispairing pleas, his mother's unyielding desapproval—made not the least dent in his resolution. No more did the immensity of his sacrifice, the ruin of his promise or the defiance of his inbred ideals of kingship carry effective weight. Even delay, the counsel of Churchill and Duff Cooper, was impossible for him: he mimicked the Churchillian rhetoric and consistently ignored the advice. His *idée fixe* had obliterated all other views from his mind. Whether his behaviour is judged wilfully obstinate or inflexibly heroic, it was certainly very extraordinary. Queen Mary marshalled five exclamation marks to express her surprise that her son should give up "the throne of this Empire to marry Mrs Simpson!!!!!"

To share her surprise is not to deprecate Edward's choice. His action will always be remembered as a magnificent assertion of unquenchable individual feeling over indifferent institutional rigidity. In the success of his marriage he gained his reward but the sentimentality with which the love theme has been treated has tended to obscure the strange harmonies underlying it. Also, hindsight lends to the oddest events an appearance of inevitablility: nothing seems so remarkable when it has happened. Today therefore it requires an effort of imagination to grasp the phenomenon of what Edward did:

> "The hallowed pleasures of a kingly life
> Abandoned for a transatlantic wife."
> *Douglas Reed*

Only by setting the abdication in the context of Edward's life as a whole can one hope to understand how he was capable of such unique behaviour. The abdication disrupted the pattern of his life so completely that it easily appears as an isolated event. But of course the strands in the King's character which caused the crisis neither originated nor disappeared in 1936. We have already noted that George V and Baldwin were able to forecast the disaster. To their prophecies a third could be added, the schoolmasterly judgement made by Chamberlain at the beginning of Edward's reign: "I do hope he pulls up his socks and behaves himself now he has such heavy responsibilities, for unless he does he will soon pull down the throne". It is time to examine the personality that could inspire such forebodings.

"But who exactly was I?"

"You have always been so sensible and easy to work with", George V wrote to Edward's brother when he married Lady Elizabeth Bowes-Lyon, "and you have always been ready to listen to any advice and to agree with my opinions about people and things, that I feel we have always got on very well together (very different to dear David)".

The parenthesis reveals the key thread in Edward's development (for he was "David" to his family)—the temperamental antithesis between him and his father. And that this letter of George V categorised readiness "to agree with my opinions about people and things" with other measures of comradeship strongly hints that the son deserves sympathy for his predicament.

One of George V's courtiers referred to his entourage as "the straightest court that ever was, and the cleanest", while the King himself was "the straightest man I ever knew". But straightness and cleanliness, laudable qualities both, are hardly foremost among the parental virtues. The undeviating directness of George V's attributed remark to Lord Derby,' My father was frightened of his mother; I was frightened of my father; and I am damn well going to see to it that my children are frightened of me", would have been small consolation to his unfortunate children; nor would those cleanly courtiers have reduced the fear he accordingly inspired. Commenting on the entry in his father's diary on the date of his birth, "at ten o'clock a sweet little boy was born", Edward hazarded that this "was the last time my father was ever inspired to apply to me that precise appellation". Possibly the child's understandable tendency to embarrass his parents by emitting shrieks of terror when confronted by Queen Victoria began the process of paternal disillusionment. At least Edward, though, did not commit the dreadful *faux pas* of his brother, Bertie, who was born on the anniversary of Prince Albert's death.

George V's background had been naval and his expression of fatherly affection was limited to the rough chaff of the wardroom. But that bluff, manly heartiness—the stentorian pronouncements of archaic opinion, the sudden explosion of rage, the tension-releasing guffaw—only increased their childish alarm. He felt that he got on with children "like a house on fire", but, if so, his own offspring were badly scorched in the blaze. They all grew up shy, and, although Edward was not afflicted with George VI's stutter, his nervous habits, noticeable even in his later Prince Charming days, of fingering his

When he abdicated it broke my heart. I used to watch him at the races . . . . he was very brave and devil-may-care. Woman in the crowd at his lying-in-state.

A popular victory. His parents congratulate the Prince
on winning a race. Prince Edward bows over his father's hand.

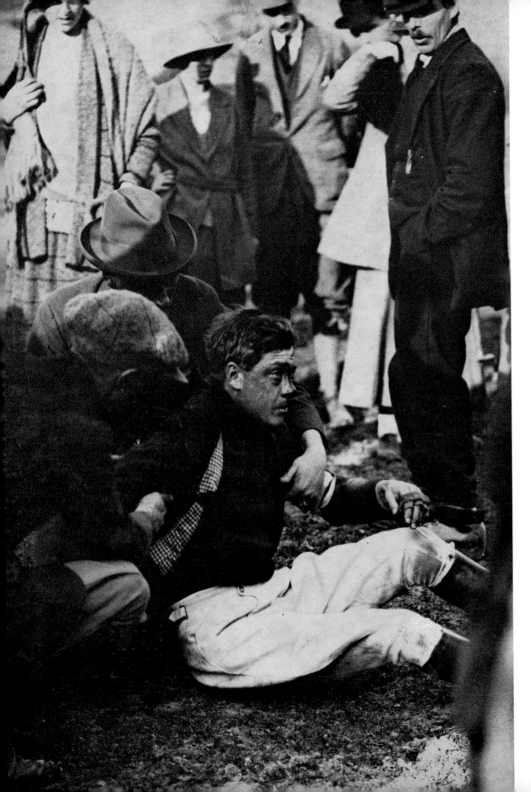

tie, shifting about in his seat, running his hands though his hair, perhaps betrayed some continuing inner unease.

But if even George V's official biographer, Harold Nicolson, was compelled to note, albeit with characteristic smoothness and discretion, that George V "failed to establish with his children, at least until they were married, those relations of equable and equal companionship that are the solace of old age", that is not to say that he lacked all affection for them, nor they for him. His failure was one of imagination rather than feeling. Queen Mary also failed to communicate her love for her sons. The constraint that began when she was pregnant with Edward ("She wants it neither remarked nor mentioned") persisted in their relations to the end of her life. This was the sadder as the charm, gaiety and intelligence which she had displayed before her marriage were closer to Edward's qualities than any of his father's granite virtues. Perhaps her pride in her son's dazzling success as Prince of Wales sprang partly from the stirrings of her own buried character. For youthful spirits had long since been sacrificed to her husband's concept of duty. "I have to remember" she once remarked of her relations with her children, "that their father is also their King."

Even when only required to remember that their father was Duke of York, she had found the responsibility appeared pressing enough to reduce considerably the sphere of maternal interest. Of course, to surrender royal children to the care of nurses, servants and tutors was customary procedure. And, to be fair, Edward has recorded that his mother would support her children when George V's severity was more than unusually unreasonable. But it seems strange that it took three years to discover that Edward's nanny was a neurotic who would pinch him and twist his arm before introducing him to the parental

But after a series of bad falls the King orders him to give up steeplechasing.

drawing room. The nanny's aim, all too easily achieved, was that his resulting screams should ensure speedy removal; apparently she hoped in this manner to poison the child's relationship with his parents.

Perhaps she succeeded; at any rate we shall have occasion to note several skirmishes between Edward and his father. Although with passing years the conscious awe of the child slowly diminished, the distance between them always remained, and later widened. No extraneous environmental factor in Edward's youth could account for this gulf, for he stayed at home with a tutor until the age of thirteen, when, his father being impressed with the beneficial effects that a naval training had produced on his own character, he became a cadet at Osborne, transferring to Dartmouth two years later. "The Navy will teach David all he needs to know", King George confidently asserted. So David learned to tie knots and splice ropes, to sail a cutter, to make signals, to use a compass, and other forms of nautical accomplishment. The life was hard and the discipline spartan, but no system could force his character into his father's mould. After the painful initial experiences Edward suffered as a result of his shyness, he began to discover that what appealed to him about service life was not the discipline but the comradeship. When, at the end of his training, he spent three months aboard the battleship *Hindustan* as a junior midshipman, an officer observed that he struck "all those about him, high and low, as a 'live thing'."

Such a description was more reminiscent of his grandfather than of his father. So it is not surprising that he always remembered Edward VII with great affection and would recall what a contrast visits to him made with his drear home life. All discipline was suddenly forgotten; nannies and tutors were shooed away by the impatient wave of a cigar; and, in his grandfather's easy indulgence and delight in pleasure, Edward discovered an alternative to his father's forbidding doctrines. For the first time he found an outlet for his natural affections. Thereafter it was Edward VII's style rather than his father's which instinctively appealed to him; and much later his interpretation of the kingly role reflected this.

George V, by contrast, convinced that distance, dignity and duty were at the root of the monarchy's strength, rigorously excluded all spontaneity from the performance of his office. His daily life was dedicated to routine and obsessed with trivial details of etiquette and dress; his courtiers were antique branches of territorial aristocracy. Such a stern concept of his position and such an inhibiting way of life came to him the more easily because they tallied with his natural inclination. For all his sterling quality, he was a conspicuously unexciting personality. "For seventeen years", his biographer despairingly writes of the period when George was Duke of York, "he did nothing at all but kill wild animals and stick in stamps." If, after his succession to the throne, he could command a greater number of birds to be killed and stamps to be stuck, he did not otherwise notably extend his interests. In 1913 he once shot over one thousand birds in a single day: "Perhaps we went a little too far today, David", he wondered. His real métier was that of blimpish country squire and naturally he was greatly loved by his subjects.

Far from mellowing with age, his conservatism became ever more deeply entrenched. His attitudes, like his dress ("He was inclined to regard any deviation from the norm of the previous decade as indicating affectation, effeminacy, or potential decadence" wrote Nicolson), remained frozen in 19th century modes. Lack of imagination prevented him from appreciating the need felt by the young for an emotional reaction after the carnage of the First World War. He had always been un-enthusiastic about any form of social life, but now he viewed the febrile gaiety of the Twenties, of which Edward took his full share, with mounting horror. Such innovations as cocktails, painted fingernails, girls riding astride, or simply going away for the weekend shocked him. Still more alarming were gambling and the new dances. "I see David continues to dance every night and most of the night too", he wrote to Queen Mary, "What a pity they should telegraph it every day, people who don't know will begin to think he is either mad or the biggest rake in Europe, such a pity." And Edward remembered: "life at Windsor for young people was a trifle overpowering to say the least. Nothing was lacking but gaiety; and the abrupt ending of the evening at 11 would leave us subdued and at a loss. One evening my brothers and I were emboldened to try to enliven the atmosphere for the younger members of the party. We had arranged with the band to wait for us in the Green Drawing Room. When my parents had gone to bed, we returned; the rugs were rolled back; and the musicians, more familiar with classical music and martial airs, made an earnest attempt to cope with outmoded foxtrots, which were as close as they could come to jazz. But our efforts to be gay were a failure. The ancient walls seemed to exude disapproval. We never tried again." Although George V's reading list included the title "Warning for Wantons", it cannot be said that his habits displayed much need of the caution.

Clearly Edward could never treat such a father as a friend, let alone a confidant. Reflecting on this, George VI said, "It was very difficult for David. My father was so inclined to go for him. I always thought that it was a pity that he found fault with him over unimportant things—like what he wore. This only put David's back up. But it was a pity that he did the

The young Prince and the elder statesman. The Prince of Wales with Lloyd George. It was Lloyd George's idea to make him a royal ambassador.

things which he knew would annoy my father. The result was that they did not discuss the important things quietly. I think that is why David did not tell him before he died that he meant to marry." Possibly indeed the relationship with Mrs Simpson, far from being a problem to be discussed, was a symbol of rebellion to be flaunted.

His mother was equally unapproachable. "David dined with me this evening, we talked a lot of nothing very intimate" is a comment that gives the tenor of their relationship. Although in 1936 Queen Mary must have had knowledge of the impending crisis the mutual inhibitions of mother and son prevented all reference to the topic. "Didn't you find it terribly warm in the Adriatic?", she queried when Edward returned from the cruise on which Mrs Simpson had accompanied him in the summer of 1936. "Her curiosity of the simple details of the voyage reminded me of how she used to talk to us when we returned from school", Edward recalled. He did not manage to tell her of his decision to marry until 16 November and his abdication (he left the country on 12 December) meant that they did not meet for nine years.

To do Queen Mary justice, however, although as George V's consort she was wounded and "humiliated" by the abdication, as Edward's mother she extended her "true sympathy for the difficult position in which you are placed". This dual response reflects at once the nature and the limits of his parents' failure: although they were starchy and unapproachable, in their hearts they were never indifferent. But as the flow of their affection was stemmed by a greater devotion to their principles, so Edward learnt to question the value of these principles. He was too close to his parents not to be affected by their values, too alienated to interpret them in the same way. Duty? Honour? Loyalty? These concepts meant as much to Edward as to his

1920. On Board HMS Renown, 'crossing the Line'. The Prince about to be shaved and ducked. King George V was not amused: *You must always remember your position and who you are.*

parents. But they did not always mean the same thing.

For Edward's ideals could never be accommodated within their narrow principles. "David is a delightful child, so intelligent, nice and friendly", thought Queen Victoria when he was nearly four, and it was a prescient judgement that remained apposite throughout his life. His flair for the casual encounter, the easy rapport he established with infinitely varied people, ensured that his perceptions came to him through a wider-angled lens than those of his parents. That is not to say they were more penetrating: the fast shutter of his mind left no time for that. But because his field of vision was broader it was correspondingly harder to assimilate his impressions into any predetermined scheme of values. Tripping lightly over the mass of material revealed, he could frame any number of relevant questions, but rarely provide any satisfactory answers. Where his father could ultimately ground his life on his absolute faith in the importance of institutions in general and monarchy in particular, Edward's essential humanity left him baffled and uncertain.

The use of that word "humanity" demands an immediate caution. It is not suggested that Edward was possessed of such burning sympathy for the common lot that he came to care nothing for the kingdom of this world. On the contrary, he enjoyed that kingdom's material offerings very much indeed. But he did possess "humanity" in a negative sense, in that he never allowed the dazzle of his position to blind him to more disturbing realities. All the aspects of his wide experience registered with him. An incident in 1919 illustrates his difference from his father in this respect. King George, on horseback, was inspecting a parade of ex-servicemen in Hyde Park. Suddenly a section broke ranks and surrounded him, demanding, in echo of Lloyd George's election slogan, "Where is the land fit for heroes?" There was no viciousness directed at the King; indeed the men sought to shake his hand. But it was clear to Edward that their message never reached its target. "After my father dismounted, he looked at me, remarking 'Those men were in a funny temper', and, shaking his head as if to rid himself of an unpleasant memory, he strode indoors." But Edward found himself thinking about the causes that had produced the disturbance.

This openness of mind and person to all experience was Edward's most attractive characteristic, and the basis of his charm. For was it not natural to be relaxed and approachable when his position appeared to him to confer no separating merit? Such an outlook by itself was irresistible enough in a prince, but its appeal was enhanced by the genuine friendliness and interest he showed in everyone he met. Once a caller who telephoned some minor official at Buckingham Palace was by mistake put through to King Edward. The man's profuse apologies were cut short by the King's cheery "Don't worry, maybe I can be of some help". Informality was always Edward's preferred mode, though it brought him many a paternal rebuke. Too many jokes were considered undignified ("The King argues that he has never made jokes in any of his public speeches"), while the wearing of a bowler hat was condemned as betraying a want of respect to the public. Edward's brave reply, which reads ironically now, was that, since the top hat was a symbol of triumphant capitalism, the public would find the bowler less offensive.

But there was more to Edward's openess of mind than just lack of stuffiness. He possessed a natural sympathy that rejected crude categories of class and nationality, and insisted on treating each person he encountered as simply a fellow human. Since he also had a happy knack with the passing remark, com-

RIGHT Touring Canada, 1919, where he captured a million hearts.

A blend of shyness and informality that gave that special charisma to the Prince of Wales; and completely won over his country's former enemies. The Prince is escorted by a Boer Commando as he rides through Worcester on a tour of South Africa, 1925.

Away on the prairie the Prince helps to round up cattle at the Bar U Ranch.

bined with an extraordinary memory for facts and faces, the devotion he aroused as Prince of Wales was almost universal. Only at George V's cheerless court were there disapproving frowns. An eighty-year old man who used to deliver milk to York Place, where Edward lived when he was Prince of Wales, and who was among the first to attend his lying-in-state, gave a good indication of why the magic was so potent: "He would always speak to me when I was delivering milk at around eight o'clock when he was coming back from riding. The last time I saw him was when he came over for his mother's funeral and he waved to me and asked me how I was, just as though he'd never been away." The contact had been of the slightest, the conversation doubtless unremarkable, but over nearly twenty years Edward had not forgotten.

Of more solid worth than the mere dispensation of charm was another expression of his humanity—his active concern for the casualties of the inter-war economic recession. Prince Charming could never forget what lay beneath the gilded crust to which he belonged. In 1932, at the nadir of the Depression, there were nearly three million unemployed: the national insurance benefit was only fifteen and threepence per week. Not before 1935 did the unemployment figure fall below two million. Edward could easily have escaped the implications of such statistics simply by continuing to do his job in the traditional manner. So many of his contemporaries turned a blind eye with less excuse. But as his imagination brought home to him the depths of the misery, so his compassion strove to alleviate it. Again and again his conscience sent him to the worst hit areas. These visits, he later recalled, could sometimes be "a severe ordeal . . . More than once I found myself walking . . . past row after row of crowded but silent benches, hearing nothing save the creak of the floorboards under my weight".

Duck shooting on the shores of Lake Qu'Appelle, Canada.
Even on private occasions he could never escape photographers.

Tarpon fishing during his tour of New Zealand. The Prince and Lord Louis Mountbatten in great form away from ceremonial and protocol. In 1972 Earl Mountbatten said, *For over 50 years he was my greatest friend.*

Touring Australia in 1920. The welcome became progressively
more boisterous, as the Australians fell under his spell.

The resentment and despair he encountered were a harsh contrast to the adulation he could have gained elsewhere with a single smile. But *he* had made the choice.

He was far too sensitive not to feel the inadequacy of his expressions of encouragement and sympathy. The words he spoke appeared to him a hollow mockery in face of such conditions. Every degradation of poverty caught his eye. Looking at a shabby becoated figure standing in a queue at a provincial soup kitchen he quietly observed "That man has no shirt on". Later that day his shock expressed itself in his despairing questions to those accompanying him—"What can I do? What can be done?"

In fact his very presence was a significant psychological contribution. Men who felt betrayed and abandoned by the Government discovered in Edward at least one symbol of official concern. The common choice of his picture as sole decoration in working men's clubs and miners' bars showed that his actions had given new strength to the cohesive power of the monarchy in British society. Nevertheless Edward felt frustrated by the powerlessness of his position. What *could* he do? First, he could help raise money. After listening to his broadcast appeal on half of distressed miners, their leader, A. J. Cook, a left-winger not given to voicing his enthusiasm for the Establishment, told Edward: "I was with two Communist friends and when your name was announced . . . they undoubtedly scoffed. But they listened to what you had to say and when you finished, with tears in their eyes they put their hands in their pockets and gave what they had on them to the fund." Secondly, Edward could use his influence in an attempt to persuade Ministers to adopt more effective means of dealing with the problems of the slump. Housing especially

The family welcome him home. The Prince always found it hard to disguise his boredon with formality.

*I danced wtth a man who danced with a girl
who danced with the Prince of Wales.*

interested him and he organised a conference to urge new suggestions on the Government.

But here he was already on dangerous ground: a member of the Royal Family could not afford to appear publicly censorious of Government inaction. Even his visits to the depressed areas worried Baldwin, and Labour politicians were equally critical of any interference with government authority. "I did not think much of it", Herbert Morrison wrote of Edward's 'Something must be done' remark in Wales, "For it was a case of a sovereign publicly expressing views on matters which were the subject of political controversy".

Morrison's cool reaction possibly owed something to his memory of an earlier clash, when, as head of the London County Council, he had refused to sell land to the Duchy of Cornwall for a housing experiment on which Edward had set his heart. It is significant that Edward made so few friends amongst politicians of either party, and there can be no question that he was singularly maladroit in his dealings with the breed. Temperamentally and intellectually impatient he suspected both the tortuous means and the inglorious ends of the political process. If one of his enthusiasms was baulked he was more likely to react destructively by sounding off loudly and tactlessly about the iniquities of politicians than constructively by attempting a modification that would render his proposal more acceptable. Persiflage came more easily than perseverance. He was not therefore an effective campaigner for any cause, especially not for those causes about which he cared passionately. The more deeply his feelings were engaged the more his disdain for compromise asserted itself. As his perception of what was right or necessary came to him with an instinctive certainty, so his reaction to any opposing view was tainted with an instinctive mistrust. To thwart his designs was to call forth the careless righteousness of the determined martyr. Regardless of the enemy's strength he would dash headlong into the conflict.

This wilfulness was closely associated with another characteristic. Edward's nature possessed a definite streak of anarchy which manifested itself in a consistent tendency to criticise authority or defy convention. Quintessentially a member of the Establishment himself, he yet naturally thought in terms of "Them" and "Us", the latter being the innocent victims of the former's stupidity or malice. Those requiring a psychological explanation for this trait need not look beyond Edward's relations with his father; indeed they had better not look beyond or they will be confronted with the problem of why Edward's brother Bertie (King George VI) emerged from the same background with an orthodox Establishment outlook. But, whatever the cause, Edward was a natural rebel. Although he was generally easy-going, the appearance or remembrance of authority immediately set his critical impulses on the alert. Certainly much of his criticism was justified but the point is that kings rarely feel impelled to publicise their resentment so unrestrainedly. His hostility to politicians is only one instance; every phase of his life provides other examples. Although in his memoirs Edward sympathised with his tutor, Mr. Hansell, for being unhappy in his job, this did not prevent him from judging his inadequecies harshly. "On looking back over those five curiously ineffectual years under him, I am appalled to discover how little I really learned. He could scarcely be said to have possessed a positive personality. If he harboured strong views about anything he was careful to conceal them. Although I was in his care on and off for more than twelve years I am

LEFT The Prince talking to World War I disabled soldiers. And to ex-service men in France. *I feel so ashamed*, he wrote, *to wear medals which I only have because of my position.*

today totally unable to recall anything brilliant or original that he said."

If, in remembering his naval college days, Edward found some individuals worthier of praise than Mr Hansell he leaves no doubt that he thought the discipline unjustifiably harsh and curriculum unprofitably narrow. One might therefore have expected Oxford to be more to his taste, but he ridiculed Dr Warren, the president of his college. "The President was a man of learning; it was therefore disillusioning to discover that the thing he most valued in the world was his connection with an obscure baronet, a fact he managed to insert into every conversation. It was generally suspected that he was obsessed with the idea of filling Magdalen with titled undergraduates; hence, whenever he beamed upon me, I was never quite certain whether it was with a teacher's benevolence or from a collector's secret satisfaction with a coveted trophy."

We shall see that in the Great War it was the men in the trenches with whom he longed to be allowed to associate himself; the rare glimpses he snatched of the horrors on the front made him contemptuous of the "General Headquarters' view" to which his position outwardly attached him. In November 1919 he was appointed to Sir John French's staff. To be cloaked in authority's life-preserving garb at such a time was intolerable to him. "We were about thirty miles from the front line, out of earshot of all but the heaviest bombardments. Sir John French had surrounded himself with older officers and friends who instinctively thought of fighting in terms of the tactics of the Boer War. They liked their food and their comforts and in the opinion of the men in the trenches were quite out of touch with what was actually happening in the line." And after the war his running battle with officialdom continued, whether with those who sought to introduce overmuch formality into his Dominion tours, or with his father's courtiers who disliked his relaxed and casual interpretation of the princely role.

Perhaps the reason such petty arguments rarely resolved themselves in good-humoured compromise was Edward's awareness that they were part of a wider contest in which he had a psychological need to win his spurs. He must have recognised that the apparatus of authority was by definition and by design obstructive of just that natural flow of feeling between man and man to which his temperament and his talents inclined him. Authority maintains itself by imposing distance with pomp and ceremony, but, as Edward's sympathy annihilated the distance, so he found the pomp and ceremony tedious. He was caught between the ideal of a common humanity to which he responded by instinct and the opposing demands of the hierarchical structure which he was expected to personify by birth.

His dislike of ceremony was strongly marked from his earliest years. "I shall look an ass", he remarked after obtaining his first dress clothes. And the same diffidence and self consciousness came to the fore in 1911 when he was invested as Prince of Wales at Carnavon Castle. He hated this occasion—"What would my navy friends say if they saw me in this preposterous rig?" Two years later, perhaps under Oxford's sceptic influence, diffidence had assumed a more aggressive guise, and after a state visit Edward wrote in his diary: "What rot and a waste of time, money and energy all these State visits are. That is my only remark to all this unreal show and ceremony." Thereafter his mind was always eager to expose the empty core of monarchical frippery. When he was King his scorn for many of the traditional public functions of a monarch often spilled over into an almost deliberate tactlessness. It was easy to sympathise with his attitude, harder to forgive his behaviour. And those

LEFT Fleet exercises in the Mediterranean. The Prince of Wales in H.M.S. Queen Elizabeth with his favourite brother Prince George, later Duke of Kent.

The dandy at the Derby.

The most devastating good looks . . . . the Prince Charming of the century. At a meet of the Beaufort Hunt in 1923.

whom he offended, being so often themselves among the lesser bastions of hierarchy, were not disposed easily to forgive an insult from the incarnate peak of their worldly values.

Take the case of the slighted debutantes. When presented at a Buckingham Palace garden party in 1936 they discovered that a sulky, bored nod was the sole acknowledgment the monarch felt inclined to give their first quavering steps in search of status. Could it be that he was unaware of the importance of the occasion? A few drops of rain provided the answer. Bestowing on the still unpresented debs "a gesture intended to express my regret over the inadvertent shower" but which seemed to those senstitive natures more like a dismissive wave, Edward hurried indoors. "It has always seemed to me that women are inclined to attach an excessive importance to these affairs", he later commented airily. Be that as it may, those ruffled maiden feelings were not much smoothed by the announcement that "those ladies . . . who, owing to the interruption of the ceremony by the weather, were unable to pass the King's presence, would be considered as having been officially presented at court".

In the same manner Edward was always liable to offend officials. Being unimpressed with his own status he was continually unmindful of the high opinion the petty dignitaries he met had of theirs, and that they looked to the King to gild their self-conceit. Thus when Edward announced that he would receive delegates from twenty city corporations together, instead of separately as formerly, the City of London delegation bitterly resented what it regarded as an intolerable snub. But sometimes the blame Edward incurred was more obviously deserved, like the occasion in September 1936 when he met Mrs Simpson off a train in Aberdeen, despite having pre-viously declined an invitation to open a hospital building there on the same day.

If, in this last case, his behaviour was indefensible, his solecisms were often mainly attributable to his ingrained, almost perverse, honesty. What he did not feel he would not act. His perhaps over-scrupulous regard for the integrity of his own feelings was especially pronounced when it gave him grounds for a conflict with the established order. For example he was never a consistent Church-goer, and his feelings were certainly not much engaged by his title of Defender of the Faith. (It is notable that this expression was missing in the Instrument of Abdication). Morally therefore he was justified in quibbling about making the formal "Declaration Insuring the Maintainance of the Protestant Succession by the Crown". But it was undeniably awkward of Edward to parade his conscience before every letter of the law, particularly if he ended, as in this case, by conceding the point. The exercise of kingship inevitably involves the swallowing and regurgitation of cant and Edward seemed unprepared to face either process.

His honesty was still more corrosive of his status when he insisted on bringing it to bear on himself. "I had been endowed with a questioning, independent mind and I found it difficult to take anything for granted, even my own position." *Especially* his own position, one must stress. For if his youthful diffidence was less obvious than that of his brother Bertie it was quite as pronounced. His estimate of his own talent was disarmingly frank for a prince. "My desires and interests were much the same as those of other people . . . and . . . however hard I tried, my capacity was somehow not appreciably above the standard demanded by the fiercely competitive world outside palace walls." No wonder he "instinctively recoiled from

RIGHT *I was absolutely appalled that such conditions could exist in our country*. The Prince after visiting the unemployed in Durham coalfields, January 1929.

FAR RIGHT *At times I could not help thinking how alone I was.*

LEFT Shooting tiger in India, 1921.

Shooting rapids in Japan. *The inscrutable faces of the Orient broke into smiles when he appeared.*

Still travelling. The Prince of Wales talks to local Yoruba
personalities in Lagos during a visit to Nigeria.

Show Biz brothers in South America, 1931.

An almost narcissistic passion for dressing up. Colonel in Chief
of Jacobs Horse, Indian Cavalry; Japanese coolie; and as a
golfer.

The Prince of Wales lights Lamps of Maintenance at the
birthday celebrations of TOC H movement, 1933.

Representing King George V at the Royal Air Force display at Hendon, 1934.

homage"; he felt he was an ordinary man and revolted against the paradox of his extraordinary position. "Remember your position and what you are", his father would intone with monotonous regularity. Always, though, came the uneasy internal response: "But who exactly was I?"

Occasionally as a young man he tried to give himself an answer to this question according to the manner born. Sudden eruptions of formality would disturb the relaxed friendliness of his disposition. When, for example, a golf professional with whom he was playing ventured to use his christian name in public, Edward immediately abandoned the game. Another incident illustrates his inner confusion about his role. Visiting his old college's junior common room at Oxford he told members to remain seated, but, when he returned, angrily demanded of the sitting undergraduates whether this was the way in which they were accustomed to treat the Prince of Wales.

But he could never conquer his diffidence or solve his identity problem by the mere assumption of privilege. The honours that came to him by virtue of his position alone were dross, and worse than dross, because they intensified his feelings of inadequacy. In the First World War his father wrote urging him to wear some honorary decorations given to him by the French and Russians. Edward's reply was firm. "I think you know how distasteful it is to me to wear these two war decorations having never done any fighting and having always been kept well out of danger! I feel so ashamed to wear medals which I only have because of my position, when there are so many thousands of gallant officers who lead a terrible existence in the trenches and who have been in battles of the fiercest kinds (many severely wounded or sick as a result) who have not been decorated. No doubt I look at this thing from a wrong and foolish point of view but this is the view I take."

Relaxed in the informal atmosphere of a 'Not Forgotten' Association Party.

The death of Kings:
ABOVE Edward VII: May 1910.
RIGHT George V: January 1936.
FAR RIGHT George VI: February 1952.

Fort Belvedere at Sunningdale, the Prince of Wales' private home, where he could entertain his own friends away from the public eye. Many of them deserted him after the abdication.

The swimming pool at the Fort, and the Prince with one of his favourite cairns. Another picture from the Prince's private collection.

He yearned to be allowed to prove himself in battle, but as always his status stood in the way of his desires. At first he could not even get to France. When his battalion (he was attached to the Guards although five inches short of the minimum six foot height) was sent abroad he was ordered to remain at home. "It was" he recalled, "a terrible blow to my pride, the worst of my life." He begged Lord Kitchener to rescind the decision—"What does it matter if I am killed, I have four brothers?" Lord Kitchener agreed with winning frankness that the possibility of Edward being killed was indeed an acceptable risk, but found that of his capture by the Germans of prohibitive alarm. Eventually Edward wrangled a staff job in France, but still he found his situation humiliating, as he confided to his diary: "Oh! to be fighting with those grand fellows and not sitting back here doing so little compared to them who are sacrificing their lives! There could be no finer death, and if one was spared how proud one would feel to have been thro it. . . ." The genuineness of these sentiments would have been attested by Edward's senior officers who were plagued by his zest for acquainting himself at close quarters with the effects of German shrapnel. "A bad shelling will always produce the Prince of Wales." On one such foray into the front line at Loos in September 1915, his chauffeur was killed, though not while Edward was in the car. He described this dangerous venture as "the most interesting four hours of my life", but he was not allowed to repeat it.

After the War his love of racing in point-to-points also reflected the same need to prove himself. Certainly the number of his falls was better testimony to his fortitude than to his horsemanship. So alarmingly dangerous was his dedication to this sport considered to be, that, especially after 1924 when he concussed himself badly, King, Queen and Prime Minister united in repeated pleas that he should give it up. Eventually, in 1928, when his father was badly ill, Edward agreed to do so. The aeroplane offered another challenge but, after making one solo flight, the landing of which struck terror into his watching instructor's heart, he gave up piloting himself.

Whatever the cause or effect of such ventures, Edward, as he grew older, became confirmed in his rejection of his father's values, and increasingly accepted himself for what he was. For this George V was largely responsible: his pig-headed insensitivity to Edward's problems (he would loudly berate his son in the presence of servants) made the breach between them irreconcilable and rebellion as much of a pleasure as a necessity. But there was also a more positive side to the development of Edward's character. Obviously the Great War had been a vital influence: although the common lot was terrible, Edward had discovered that he was only happy to the extent that he could share it. We have seen that this was frustratingly little, but even so at times he came nearer than ever before to shedding the separating distinction of royalty. In the face of that universal catastrophe artificial barriers between individuals naturally relaxed and he was for the first time able to make friends on easy terms. This new freedom was symbolised by his choice of riding a bicycle in France instead of using the proffered staff car. The thrill of the war experience was short-lived but the depth of the impression remained.

Then the brilliant success he achieved in the Twenties with his informal style as Prince of Wales inevitably gave him a more aggressively confident view of his own personality. His diffidence was not so much conquered as absorbed, becoming an integral part of his image of himself as an ordinary man. For how could diffidence trouble a prince who had become accustomed to bask in the adulation of Empire? Equally,

though, how could such a man really be ordinary? On the one hand, he had only to look at the cheering crowds to know that his human gifts were as important as his father's principles; and he had only to look at his father to strengthen that belief. The question "Who exactly was I?" was thus unequivocably answered in favour of his "ordinary" self. On the other hand such a solution to his internal identity conflict only sharpened the external one between his character and his position, for his ability to compromise with those aspects of monarchy he found repugnant had been reduced. While he was uncertain he was malleable; now he was secure he was unshakeable.

If Edward could not bend his personality to his office, perhaps he could reconcile the conflict by bending his office to his personality. As early as 1918 he had written to his father emphasising the need for post-war monarchy to keep "in the closest possible touch with the people". Might he achieve this end as king by bringing the same informal style that had earned him so much popularity as Prince of Wales to his new task? Could he reject the life denying protocol of his father's court and create another, more broadly based order, reflective of his own talents and interests? Would he be able to enforce his insistence on maintaining a distinction between his public and private life? To the last question the abdication provided a definite negative—and so the others remained unanswered.

But his first experiments were not encouraging. Edward soon discovered that being Prince of Wales and being King were very different occupations. As King he had only to be photographed walking out of Buckingham Palace with an umbrella to elicit shocked cries of dismay. At Sandringham his decision to put the clocks back to normal Greenwich time, instead of keeping them half an hour fast, as had been George V's practice, seemed ominously revolutionary to the staff.

Edward's reduction of the number of servants and his habit of having informal suppers at Balmoral also caused alarm. But if the courtiers were outraged, his brief reign did contain evidence that Edward had not lost his popular touch: his two day visit to the Navy at Portsmouth in November was a brilliant success.

In later years Edward judged that, since he was determined to be king on his own terms, some kind of clash with the old order was inevitable. He would have done better, however, to have worn down opposition with a series of small victories instead of challenging them immediately to one all-decisive combat on such uncertain ground. He could have lulled officials by assiduous attention to routine duties instead of frustrating them with his inattention to paper-work. But patience came no more easily to Edward than compromise.

Nor was there much incentive for him to exercise it: we have seen how he resented the lack of effective power which his position conferred. "Why should he work?", asked Bagehot in 1867, regarding the constitutional monarch with prophetic insight. "It is true that he will lose the quiet and secret influence which in the course of years industry would gain for him; but an eager young man, on whom the world is squandering its luxuries and its temptations, will not be much attracted by the distant prospect of a moderate influence over dull matters." And in 1966 Edward echoed these sentiments. "Being a monarch . . . can surely be one of the most confining, the most frustrating, and over the duller stretches, the least stimulating jobs open to an educated, independent minded person."

It is the irony of Edward's life that this attitude sprang out of his better qualities as much as his failings. Had he been dull, pompous and self-satisfied, how much simpler he would have

LEFT This picture, taken in 1935 with a concealed camera, is believed to be the first press photograph taken of the Prince with Mrs. Simpson.

found his task, and, moreover, how dazzled those debutantes, how impressed those city corporations, would have been. Or had he accepted his father's narrow ideals, how obsequiously the courtiers, how reverently the politicians would have fawned. But that he could never do. For Edward, Duty concerned obligations to humanity as well as to institutions; Honour meant the refusal to compromise that creed rather the need to repress it; and Loyalty was owed to feelings as much as to systems.

Such a code sounds splendid in theory, but, interpreted by Edward's wilful and anarchic nature, it cut his personality loose from the moorings of status as cleanly as status had severed him from the life that he longed to lead. Almost by definition royalty must be isolated, but generally, theirs is the isolation of the clan, justified by the clan sense of duty and rendered supportable by the security and privilege which the oiled wheels of monarchical machinery convey. Edward's nature was in revolt against clan, clan sense of duty, security, privilege, and machinery. He was condemned to the fate of outsider.

"Something alien, something apart"

Edward might have been especially fashioned to be the prisoner of love. Naturally warm-hearted and affectionate, his outsider's plight and his family background made it abnormally important for him to satisfy the normal desire to love and be loved. For he had not only to find an outlet for his emotions; he had also to find a support in his isolation. It is impossible to appreciate the extent to which he depended on love for this support without first understanding that he lacked both the opportunities and the inner resources to meet his needs in any other way. Before he married there was never anything stable or impregnable in his life.

The uncertain course of his career, no less than the conflicts described in the last chapter, had left him rootless and undirected. Although the education of royal children presents difficult problems that recur in every generation, Edward's early life could surely have been ordered on more consistent principles. If George V had formed any definite educative plan for his son it is not now discernible. It cannot have been easy for a boy who had been privately tutored as a privileged recluse until he was thirteen to be suddenly plunged into the rough equality of Osborne. No wonder he was shy and bewildered to begin with, but no sooner had he started to enjoy being a naval cadet than he was snatched away to Oxford. Here the same lack of purpose was evident, for there was no more intention that Edward should take a normal degree than there had been that a naval training should lead to a naval career. The sudden change of tack towards Oxford had been taken on Mr Hansell's advice and "what I had to say to the poor man . . . was nobody's business". Again he had to establish himself in an alien setting; and he was not aided by a streak of obstinate independence that made him refuse to befriend Lord Stanley whom George V had arranged should accompany him to Oxford. Rebelliousness not antipathy was the cause for later, in the war, the two came to like each other well.

So Edward grew up without the opportunity to attach strong loyalties to any particular way of life outside the royal role which he was to react against, while the lack of continuously shared experience in youth made it difficult for him to consolidate any friendships. As we have seen, the Great War provided a temporary solution to these problems but afterwards his life as Prince of Wales presented the old dilemma, albeit in less obvious guise. Certainly, he was now committed to a job, but the nature of that job made him essentially a spectator rather than a participant. He was required to meet a great variety of men and to display a keen interest in all manner of occupations, but the meetings were always casual and the interest necessarily dilettante. The need to appeal to all men left him closely associated with none.

Only amongst his own staff, who shared his isolating task, did he make real friends. There was Major "Fruity" Metcalfe, who had been Edward's A.D.C. on his Indian tour and later joined his permanent staff as equerry. "Of all my friends", Edward wrote "it was he alone, with his informal and expansive Irish nature, who behaved towards me, not as though I were a Prince, but as though I were an ordinary human being like himself." "Fruity" certainly had an appreciative audience. When he struck a match on the sole of Edward's boot the Prince professed himself "amused and delighted" by this "lighthearted and characteristic gesture". Then there was another friend made during Edward's Indian tour, his Military Secretary, Colonel Rivers Worgan, "a dashing cavalry officer who might have galloped straight of the pages of Kipling. He was always immaculately turned out and, if a trifle pompous, was an eight goal polo player and a very brave soldier." Colonel Worgan was later to take these talents to a nudist colony, where doubtless his turn-out was equally immaculate. And Edward's "constant companion in things pertaining to the lighter side of my princely role" was Brigadier-General G. F. Trotter who passed on his rather unspecific view that life should be lived to the full. But these apart, Edward's male friends were astonishingly scarce. After the abdication, Archbishop Lang, himself no slouch in the snobbery stakes, accused Edward of moving "within a social circle whose standards and ways of life are alien to the best instincts of his people". "I don't know who the Archbishop meant as the late

King had no friends" one M.P. commented. This remark was fashioned with considerable malicious finesse, since it was made to be overheard by Chips Channon whose social career had reached its zenith when he entertained King Edward to dinner. Even Chips, though, was compelled to admit "It is terribly true".

If Edward had not a wide enough circle of friends, nor a sufficiently absorbing job, no more had he the intellectual resources to enable him to adapt to his outsider status. His brain was quick enough but possessed neither the depth nor the staying power to cultivate any serious mental interest let alone to formulate a self-sufficient philosophy of life. It was perhaps natural that as a child Edward should have disliked being dragged around cathedrals, but strange that forty years later he could still ridicule his tutor's interest in architecture as an "unique hobby". At Oxford he sought refuge from the printed page in all kinds of unacademic endeavour: he learnt to ride, he went beagling, he played tennis, golf, football, and roulette, he joined the O.T.C., he took up the banjo. His college president's prediction—"Bookish he will never be: not a 'Beauclerk', still less a 'British Solomon' "—was not therefore overbold, especially as it was speedily followed by a testimonial to more nebulous Oxonian accomplishment. "All the time he was learning more everyday of men, gauging character, watching its play, getting to know what Englishmen are like both individually and still more in the mass. . . ."

Notwithstanding the acquisition of such knowledge, his tastes were always more for gloss than for substance. He liked the chic and the contemporary: new clothes, the latest dances, popular music, a slickly designed cigarette lighter—these were the sort of things that took his fancy. In particular any innovation from America was likely to intrigue him, the more

especially as it was certain to arouse his father's distrust.

This natural inclination towards the superficial was perfectly compatible with his social concern. Where the first was a product of the brain, the second was rooted in his feelings. For Edward's humanity was never underpinned by any intellectual theory. He was not a radical in the sense that he wanted to change the order of society. Certainly he was moved by the suffering of the unemployed, but *what* "must be done" could never consistently absorb his attention, let alone lend purpose to his life. In his memoirs he gave a "fond salute to the elegant pleasures that were available in my youth under capitalism." The General Strike found him firmly on the employers' side; although his position compelled him to appear outwardly neutral he lent his car to help deliver the *British Gazette*, the Government newspaper. He shared the view of those who felt that the Strike was "terribly wrong, something contrary to British traditions" and thought the upper and middle classes "put up a first-class show" helping to keep the special services running. Edward believed in charity not socialism and for this reason his charity was often resented by socialists. And if he had anything in common with his father it was a hatred and terror of communism. It was this fear on which Hitler cleverly played when Edward met him after the abdication.

Edward's views on foreign policy, and his attempts, in ways that even Queen Victoria would never have countenanced, to enforce these views on the Government, highlight his intellectual limitations. His unwillingness to read Foreign Office dispatches and his consequent ignorance of the manoeuvres of diplomacy did not prevent his blundering into international affairs with any number of instant insights. Like many mentally shallow people, he prided himself on being a realist— "Heaven spare us from idealists, they cause all the trouble"—

Edward VIII of Great Britain, Ireland and the British Dominions beyond the seas, Emperor of India. He reigned for 325 days.

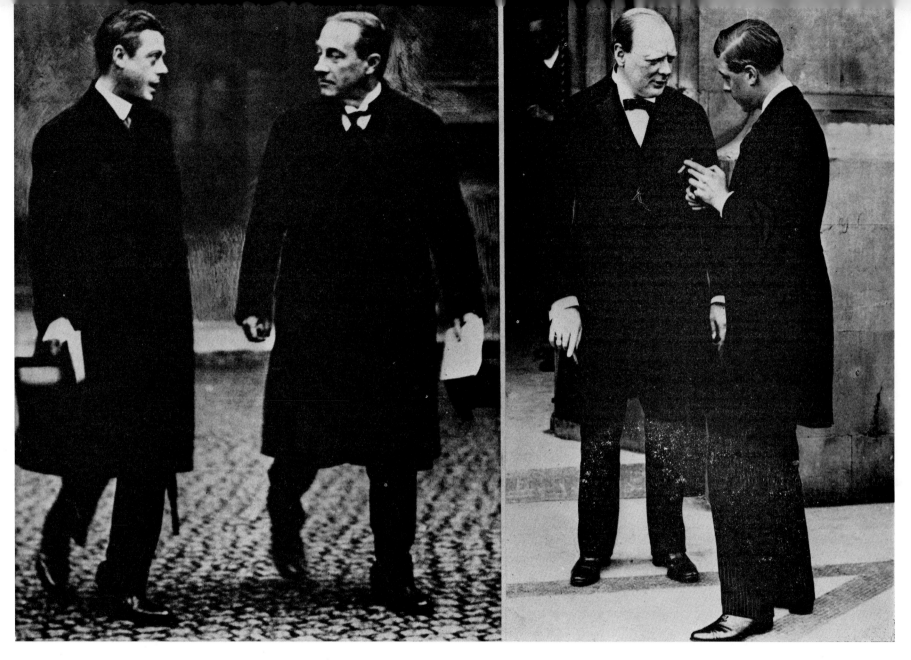

At the time of his accession Baldwin said of Edward VIII,
He has the secret of youth in the prime of age, and Churchill
prophesied that *his personality will not go uncherished down the ages*.

and was thus full of blustery contempt for the League of Nations. In particular he derided its efforts to stop Mussolini's despicable Abyssinian venture. So when the expelled Emperor, Haile Selassie, appeared in London, Edward flatly refused to comply with the Foreign Secretary's suggestion that it would be a popular gesture to receive him at Buckingham Palace. "Popular with whom?", he demanded, "certainly not with the Italians". He based this attitude on the importance of not driving Mussolini into Hitler's steel embrace, but on other occasions showed no such sensitivity to the danger from Germany.

There is no evidence that Edward admired either Hitler or the Nazis, although he may have been fascinated, even perhaps wistfully envious, of the power Hitler wielded in comparison with his own impotence. In his memoirs he recalls that the Fuhrer "struck me as a somewhat ridiculous figure, with his theatrical posturings and his bombastic pretensions". At the time, however, he certainly overestimated the extent to which Hitler was amenable to reason; and even felt it worthwhile to send him a telegram in September 1939, asking him not to go to war. But whatever his views on Hitler, Edward had always been sympathetically inclined towards Germany. These feelings derived from a visit he made to that country in 1913; "I ended in liking Germany so much that I left planning another trip in 1914".

That was not to be, but his favourable impression survived the experience of the Great War. The Kaiser had thought Edward "a young eagle, likely to play a big part in European affairs because he is far from being a pacifist". In the 1930s, however, Edward's influence was all on the side of appeasement. When Hitler occupied the Rhineland in March 1936, Anthony Eden, the Foreign Secretary, found that the King's

persuasions were urgently directed against any hostile retort. Later that year Eden told the Czech ambassador that the Foreign Office had become increasingly concerned by Edward's interventions, and even added (so the ambassador understood) that there were means of forcing him to abdicate if this continued. But abdication was a two-edged weapon. Hesse recalled that Edward told the German ambassador, who had asked the king to intervene in the Rhineland crisis: "I sent for the Prime Minister and gave him a piece of my mind. I told the old so-and-so that I would abdicate if he made war. There was a frightful scene. But you needn't worry. There won't be a war." And when Duff Cooper arrived at Fort Belvedere shortly after making a strong protest against the German action in the Rhineland the King's face was "heavy with displeasure".

Naturally the Nazis were quick to see the opportunities presented by Edward's apparent sympathy with the German cause. Ribbentrop claims that he turned down Hitler's offer of the Foreign Ministry in Berlin so that he could come to London as ambassador to exploit the situation. Gossip soon circulated that he was a friend of Mrs Simpson; in fact they only met at a couple of dinner parties and she had disliked him. But the Foreign Office was seriously alarmed. The official papers sent to Fort Belvedere where Mrs Simpson often stayed with Edward were carefully screened. The King, apparently, had become a security risk.

So far had Edward's realism led him. But in following his foreign policy blunders to this melancholy end, we have digressed from the main argument, that Edward's intellectual abilities were not sufficient to sustain him in his isolation.

The traditional escape for the outsider is travel. Being himself attached to no particular way of life, he is the more likely to find facets to which he can respond in other life-styles. By travelling he can discover an attraction, savour it, and move on before other, less congenial elements began to grate. It is not therefore surprising that Edward's Dominion tours were the most successful part of his career. He went to Canada in 1919, Australia and New Zealand in 1920, India in 1921-2 and Africa in 1925, this last tour being combined with a visit to South America.

Altogether on these journeys he covered 150,000 miles, which indicates a crowded schedule since he claimed no assistance from the aeroplane. But Edward was brimming with energy, and time and again he would round off an exhausting day by dancing half the night, and not always with the wives of officials.

Almost everywhere he was rapturously received and in Canada and Australia he was mobbed as unrestrainedly as a modern pop-star, which soon brought George V's sense of dignity snapping into action. But Edward revelled in the experience and the words in which he recalled its intoxicating effect were significant: "the Canadians in their kindly enthusiasm almost convinced me that they liked me for myself, an act of open-heartedness that did my ego no end of good". One time in Canada he was actually lifted from his horse and passed over the heads of the crowd; and his right hand became so swollen as a result of the pumping it received that he "retired it temporarily from Imperial service and offered the left instead." The Australian welcome was quite as boisterous. Touching the Prince of Wales became a national obsession and "touching" often entailed a staggering thump or even a blow on Edward's head with a rolled up newspaper. But his style was irresistible, as when his train carriage overturned and he emerged from the wreckage to thank his hosts for throwing in

something not on the official programme. Only in India was there a note of discord, for Gandhi had ordered his followers to boycott the Imperial visit. Nevertheless, Edward's appeal often triumphed over nationalist sentiment, although it was, as the Chief Secretary reported, "noteworthy that where the ringleaders were arrested before H.R.H.'s arrival (i.e. in all the provinces except Bombay and Madras) there was no rioting".

Edward thoroughly deserved the triumph of these Imperial tours. At a time when high society in London found the gaucherie of Dominion manners more remarkable than the strength of their devotion to the mother country, while even the enthusiasm of the Empire-builders was on the wane, he identified himself totally with the people and aspirations of the countries which he visited. "I'm rubbing it in that although not actually Canadian born I'm a Canadian in mind and spirit and come here as such and not as a stranger or a visitor and that goes down well!" Such an approach was all the more effective because it was genuine. Edward truly belonged to no society and could therefore associate himself with wherever he happened to be—provided he did not remain there overlong. This was a talent of inestimable worth in a prince, for by the 1920s the ties which attached the Dominions to Britain were in practice so minimal (in 1923 the Dominions' independence in foreign affairs was officially recognised; they had long had control over internal affairs) that the symbolic importance of the Crown, as the sole remaining link, was greatly enhanced. Edward strengthened the emotional bond while all others were being cut away; it was the greatest achievement of his life.

Although it was Edward's rootlessness that made him such a fine ambassador, travel only provided a temporary palliative for his basic problem. He remained an outsider. Possibly his success even had a dangerously delusive effect on him person-

RIGHT One of his visit's to London's East End slums. His social conscience was 20 years ahead of his time.

ally, causing him to exaggerate the power of his popularity. Certainly, though, his father was not over-impressed; he still refused to show Edward any official despatches, being as unyielding in this respect as Victoria had been with Edward VII. This deliberate slight was just one more way in which George V alienated his son from the royal role, although no prince was ever in such need of sympathetic understanding.

From 1930 on Edward's search for stability assumed a more material guise: he acquired a home. After the War he had taken York Place, St James' Palace, as his London home, manfully resisting Queen Mary's persistent efforts to move him into Marlborough House. But he longed for a country home and in Fort Belvedere, near Virginia Water, he found his ideal. A "pseudo-Gothic hodge-podge", it would certainly not have appealed to architectural connoisseurs like Mr Hansell, but Edward became entirely captivated: "soon I came to love it as I loved no other material thing". His main passion was for the garden in which he himself worked furiously at the weekends, often dragooning his guests into sharing the exhausting labour, "to which", as he mildly phrased it, "some of them were unaccustomed". Whether as a result of these exertions, or from the less frenetic efforts of the gardeners during the week, the grounds were soon in trim shape. To this "enchanted Fort", in January 1932, came Ernest Simpson and his wife Wallis; later, in 1939, she returned with another husband and found the enchantment less magical. "The lawn was overgrown; the garden in which we had spent so many happy hours together had become a mass of weeds; and the house itself, shuttered, damp and dark, was slowly decaying."

That was only a small part of the price which Edward's need for love was to exact. Obviously, though, it was no sudden bewitchment that separated Edward from his throne; Mrs Simpson's first visit to the Fort was nearly five years before the abdication and more than one year after their first meeting. This had taken place in 1930, at Burrough Court, near Melton Mowbray, and, according to Edward's memoirs, Mrs Simpson immediately made a bold conversational strike with her reply to his small talk about Americans missing central heating: "I am sorry, Sir, but you have disappointed me.... Every American woman who comes to your country is always asked that same question. I had hoped for something more original from the Prince of Wales." Such an exchange sounds inherently improbable at that stage, though it is in keeping with Mrs Simpson's style. Possibly Edward unconsciously transposed a later remark to that first encounter. Certainly his wife firmly corrected the date given by his account from 1931 to 1930, and has no recollection of the central heating conversation. "The truth is that I was petrified". The conflict between their versions of the first meeting strongly suggests that in reality it made no deep impression on Edward. The reason is that Mrs Simpson did not appear in his life as a long-awaited first love. Rather he slowly discovered in her an alternative to a woman he had never been able wholly to win. For many years before he met Mrs Simpson Edward had been devotedly in love with another married woman, Mrs Dudley Ward.

This affair, which lasted for 17 years, only became widely known in June 1972, when extracts from Frances Donaldson's biography of Edward were serialised in the *Sunday Telegraph*. (The book, to be published in 1973, is eagerly awaited.) Edward's liaison with Mrs Dudley Ward began with a chance encounter in 1917. During an air raid she sought shelter in an open house in Belgrave Square. Inside there was a party and the hostess (by an astonishing coincidence Ernest Simpson's sister) invited her to join the other guests sheltering in the

LEFT Buckingham Palace. *I did not like Buck House, it was so cold and draughty ... somehow I had the feeling I might not be there long.*

Edward VIII speaking after unveiling the Canadian War Memorial at Vimy Ridge, France.

An incident on Constitution Hill when a man hurled a revolver at the King. At the head of his troops Edward VIII rode calmly on.

The King and Mrs Simpson together by the Adriatic, summer 1936.

On board the yacht *Nahlin* which the King had chartered for the Adriatic cruise.

cellar. There, in the dark, Mrs Dudley Ward found herself next to an agreeable young man who chatted away to her all through the raid. Apparently she had no idea who he was, though he did say, in answer to her question, that he lived in London and Windsor. Only when the party resumed did she discover that he was the Prince of Wales. Their meeting next day was less fortuitous.

Edward had emerged from his restricting royal background shy and uncertain with women, and no-one could have been better qualified than Mrs Dudley Ward to put him at his ease. In all respects she presented an alluring contrast to his parents' ideals. It was not just that she was deliciously attractive, though her slim, boyish figure drove would-be emulators to the edge of starvation. She was gay, friendly, funny, sharp, unimpressed by social or other distinctions. Above all, she possessed that physical and mental confidence that instinctively appealed to Edward who felt so keenly the lack of it in himself. He always preferred the security offered by experienced women to the challenge of innocence. His ardent feelings, so long imprisoned, rushed out and enveloped her and it was more than fifteen years before he could recall them. During all that time he would visit her almost daily when he was in London and if they could not meet he would always telephone. But this consistently punctual address never slaked the fervour of his devotion.

For her part, she was fond of him and wanted to help him, but she could never fully answer the call of his heart. Completely devoid of social ambition, she acted from kindness as much as from love. Her discretion was therefore absolute and she did nothing to encourage Edward's suggestions, portents of his future action, that he should throw up his position and go away with her. As she did not feel possessive or jealous if he

LEFT *Something must be done*. Edward's visit brought a gleam of hope to the poor and unemployed. This picture shows him in the Rhondda Valley, 1932.

The news breaks in London. 3 December, 1936.

I told Mr Baldwin I would marry Mrs Simpson on the throne or off. Baldwin leaves 10, Downing Street to break the news to the House of Commons.

The King's party was more demonstrative than numerous.

INSTRUMENT OF ABDICATION

I, Edward the Eighth, of Great
Britain, Ireland, and the British Dominions
beyond the Seas, King, Emperor of India, do
hereby declare My irrevocable determination
to renounce the Throne for Myself and for
My descendants, and My desire that effect
should be given to this Instrument of
Abdication immediately.

In token whereof I have hereunto set
My hand this tenth day of December, nineteen
hundred and thirty six, in the presence of
the witnesses whose signatures are subscribed.

SIGNED AT
FORT BELVEDERE
IN THE PRESENCE
OF

Edward RI

Albert

Henry

George

---

appeared to forsake her temporarily for other women, so she wanted to remain free herself. It was this determined independence that he finally found impossible to take; he could not bear to see her with other men. The end, which came in 1934, was bitter, and, though Edward had known her younger daughter since she had been a little girl, he snubbed her cruelly when she was presented at court after the break. Mrs Dudley Ward herself he never saw again.

This denouement was all the sadder because she had been such an excellent influence. Publicly never assertive, in private she sustained and moulded him. Her kindly mockery penetrated his reserve and assuaged his loneliness. Most important, because she was blessed with so much humanity herself, she was able to foster that quality in Edward, not only in their own relationship but also by turning his mind towards the sufferings of the poor. Edward has rightly been given praise for his visits to the depressed areas, but Mrs Dudley Ward should claim a share of it. She was herself dedicated (if so stern a word can be applied to so spontaneous a person) to social work, and one of her ventures was to found clubs for children in the East End. She called them the Feathers Clubs, after the Prince of Wales' feathers, although that was not realised at the time. Edward took a keen interest in these clubs, going to see them, contributing money and encouraging others to do likewise.

Although Mrs Dudley Ward held first place in Edward's affections throughout the period between the Great War and the advent of Mrs Simpson, she did not exclude all other women. There were two worthy of note, one because Edward might have married her, the other because she provided the connection with Mrs Simpson.

At the end of the war Edward fell in love with Lady Rosemary Leveson-Gower, to the extent certainly of contemplating, possibly of actually proposing, marriage. She was the daughter of the Duke of Sutherland and so, one might have thought, a suitable enough match, besides being equally well qualified by character. Two things, however, barred the way. First, Edward's parents behaved as though the union of the heir to the throne with merely ducal blood would pollute the clear Hanoverian stream; secondly, Lady Rosemary, perhaps influenced by this haughty attitude, could not bring herself to face the possibility of becoming Queen. Retrospectively George V's cold reaction to the prospect of this marriage must count among the most disastrous of all his mistakes in his dealings with his son.

The other woman, Lady Furness, was not of herself especially important in Edward's life, though she did not stint her prose in describing her "royal romance". The affair had its apotheosis on a trip the Prince made in 1930 to East Africa, where, in that "tropic African night . . . his arms about me were the only reality; his words of love my only bridge to life . . ." Lady Furness even found herself being "swept from the accustomed moorings of caution", but by day the pleasures of photography were scarcely less exciting: "I got a wonderful, though rather harrowing, shot of a native boy being clawed by one of the lions . . . In spite of my horror at the accident and the shaking of my hands, I kept my Bell & Howell trained on the scene—and ended the day with a remarkably good sequence. I am sorry that I lost these films in one of the Blitz raids on London."

This woman had a sister who knew the Simpsons, and so the fateful introduction came about. Lady Furness, however, remained blithely insensitive to the danger. Before she went to America in January 1934 she felt so concerned for the desolation that her absence would cause the Prince that she told Mrs Simpson: "You look after him for me while I'm away. See that he does not get into any mischief". When she returned after two months Mrs Simpson's "cold, defiant glance" showed her that at least the first part of her instructions had been obeyed.

In some ways Mrs Simpson's appeal was similar to that of Mrs Dudley Ward. Like her, she was charming, vivacious, quick-witted, confident and gay. She had not worn black stockings, she once boasted, since giving up the Can-Can. Such light-hearted flippancy, combined with a taste for provocative banter, soon cut through Edward's reserve, but having thus reached him with amusing trivia, she was able to establish a more serious rapport. Edward enjoyed sharing their mutual tastes in dancing, music, fashion and gossip, but he soon discovered that the problems of his life and his attempts to solve them were also matters that engaged her ready sympathy. And not only sympathy: she possessed an independence which enabled her to act as a guide. Most people who knew them both (and hardly anyone who did not) agreed that she was good for him. It was not her fault if his obsession with her made him inattentive to routine business. On the contrary, as Lord Monckton recalled, she "undoubtedly kept him up to the mark in physical fitness and in interest in public life." And again, "To him she was the perfect woman. She insisted that he should be at his best and do his best at all times, and he regarded her as his inspiration. It is a great mistake to assume that he was merely in love with her in the ordinary physical sense of the term. There was an intellectual companionship, and there is no doubt that his lonely nature found in her a spiritual comradeship." That is true but the surface attraction remained important. Mrs Simpson was not beautiful, but she possessed just the smart contemporary appeal which attracted

Edward and even—supreme accolade—earned the seal of Lady Diana Cooper's approval. "Wallis is admirably correct and chic. Me bang wrong", Lady Diana discovered on a visit to the Fort. Correct and chic Wallis certainly was; nothing in her background or her career had persuaded her to undervalue the importance of money or social position.

Mrs Simpson once told Chips Channon that she disliked her fellow Americans (" 'They have no air', she said, and she likes air"), yet many of her own qualities were distinctively American, and all the more likely to appeal to Edward on that account. When he first visited America after his Canadian tour in 1919 he had been given a tumultuous reception. On that occasion the Americans' zest for life, their unrestrained friendliness, their lack of social pomposity and their extravagant humour all delighted him and this favourable impression strengthened over the years. This was far from being an enthusiasm shared by his father's court or by smart English society, which has always, and with reason, feared the fresh transatlantic breeze. Edward had known at least two shining exceptions to this reprehensible rule in Winston Churchill and Mrs Dudley Ward, but the more fastidious Harold Nicolson expressed the general attitude to Mrs Simpson when he judged that "the upper classes mind her being an American more than they mind her being divorced. The lower classes do not mind her being an American but loathe the idea that she has two husbands living already." So the *Morning Post* sought to calm its well-bred readers fears by suggesting that Mrs Simpson might have been descended from a knight who came over to England with the Conqueror.

Such genealogical reassurance had been rendered necessary because of the vital respect in which Mrs Simpson differed from Mrs Dudley Ward: she wanted to marry Edward. Moreover she possessed the will, which needed to be very considerable, to maintain her resolve in the face of the fury that was unleashed. Cynics say that she was sustained by the hope of becoming queen. Obviously she must have dreamed of this and in her memoirs she was undisguisedly candid about his allure. "Over and beyond the charm of his personality and the warmth of his manner he was the open sesame to a new and glittering world that excited me as nothing in my life had done before." But surely she was too intelligent to have been much deceived about her chances. "Well, anyway, a tiara is one of the things I shall never have", she remarked at a dinner party in November 1936. At her wedding Walter Monckton graciously informed her "that most people in England disliked her very much because the Duke had married her and given up his throne, but that if she made him, and kept him, happy all his days, all that would change; but that if he were unhappy nothing would be too bad for her. She took it all very simply and kindly, just saying: 'Walter, don't you think I have thought of all that? I think I can make him happy.' "

For Edward there was even more at stake, both materially and emotionally. Prince Christopher of Greece saw him with Mrs Simpson at a Buckingham Palace Ball in 1935 (incidentally the only occasion she met George V; neither made a new friend) and later remembered: "The Prince of Wales scarcely left her side all evening, despite the fact that some of the most beautiful women in Europe were doing their best to attract his attention. He appeared never even to notice them. He was in love as it is given to men and women to love only once in a lifetime." Prince Christopher was wrong about the uniqueness of the experience, in Edward's life at least, but his judgement was not otherwise amiss: everybody who saw them together after 1934 reached the same conclusion. Once again Edward

Wedding Day at the Chateau de Condé, France. June 3rd, 1937.

had given all the heart, but this time the gift was returned, a benediction which appeared all the greater because previously it had been so long denied. When his past life had produced no alternative security, it was natural for him to see in Mrs Simpson a last chance to escape from his isolation, or at least a last chance to secure someone with whom to share his outsider's fate. But still his position, that cursed position as it seemed to him, which had thwarted his nature at every turn in his life, stood in his way. It had caused the problem and now it prevented the solution. George V's death removed the last restraint. Petty acts of insubordination would no longer suffice; the issue was so vital to him that it called for a decisive challenge.

That realisation let loose all the anarchic gremlins in his character. If they wanted someone like his father, he told Lord Monckton, there was always the Duke of York. For himself, he would not deviate from his self-destructive course and that perverse honesty of his directed the way. It would be humbug, he insisted, to avoid the issue by keeping Mrs Simpson as his mistress without marrying her. No, he would not delay, because "to have gone through the Coronation service while harbouring in my heart a secret intention to marry contrary to the Church's tenets would have meant being crowned with a lie on my lips". No, he would not be discreet because that appeared a species of dishonesty. "Discretion is a quality which, though useful, I have never particularly admired", he loftily pronounced.

So, when Mrs Simpson came to dinner with her husband at York Place to meet the Prime Minister, and without her husband to another royal dinner party shortly afterwards, her presence and her husband's absence were advertised in the Court Circular. So, when she accompanied the King on the

Nahlin cruise that summer, photographs of them together were plastered all over the foreign press. ("Do you think you could possibly get the King to at least put his shirt on until we get out of sight of the Greeks?", Lady Diana Duff Cooper pleaded with Mrs Simpson. But she had met her match. "After you, my dear Diana. If this were my President, I might. But you have had more experience at dealing with kings.") And so, after the *Nahlin* cruise, the Court Circular recorded, in place of the previous autumnal visits of Archbishop Lang to his dear friend George V, the arrival of Mrs Simpson and her friends at Balmoral. Lang found some compensation in an invitation from the dear Duke and Duchess of York and doubtless some comfort in the reflection that "it was strange to think of the destiny which may be awaiting the little Elizabeth, at present second from the throne". His speculations were vindicated for neither Edward nor Mrs Simpson were ever to visit Balmoral again and today it seems odd to think of the two of them being sheltered by those severe walls.

This record of Edward's folly reflects his unbalanced mental state. The only reality whose claims he acknowledged was Mrs Simpson, because only she offered the emotional security he craved. He was thus incapable of forming a rational plan of campaign. "I'll manage it somehow", he assured Mrs Simpson of their prospective marriage, but his optimism was unsupported by resourcefulness. Moreover his scrupulousness further inhibited him by ensuring that his respect for constitutional propriety survived unscathed amid the ruin he inflicted. He remained zealously protective of the dignity of the Crown even while undermining his own occupancy of the position. He never attempted to overrule the Prime Minister's advice or to do anything that would divide the nation. "Our cock won't fight", complained Lord Beaverbrook, who had been sum-moned from New York to advise the King. But, in contrast to Edward, Beaverbrook's main motive was mischievous and political; he wanted, as he nicely phrased it, "to bugger Baldwin". That this should have been the dominant purpose of the King's adviser powerfully suggests his lack of real friends. The exception was Churchill whose romantic devotion to monarchy made him an ardent champion of Edward. Aneurin Bevan met him at Beaverbrook's house, weeping copiously into his whisky, and mourning "I never thought the time had come when a Churchill must desert his King". "Oh, its only the second occasion in history", Bevan cheerfully returned, recalling the first Duke of Marlborough's dubious early career. None the less Churchill made great sacrifices for Edward, bringing his career to its lowest point when he was howled down in the House of Commons for continuing to advocate the King's cause. But his efforts were all in vain; he had failed to grasp either the mood of the nation or the irrevocable nature of Edward's decision. With characteristic generosity Churchill later admitted that Baldwin had been right over the abdication. In truth, the King was beyond all assistance.

Indeed, Edward was so fixed in his determination to marry whatever the consequences that he was able to maintain an extraordinary personal calm, notwithstanding the rashness of his actions. While his life cracked into pieces, his manners remained impeccable and in company he was even gay and cheerful. At one of his worst moments, when Mrs Simpson was about to leave for Cannes on 3 December, Lord Monck-ton's seventeen-year-old daughter lunched at Fort Belvedere. She recalled how thoughtfully Mrs Simpson tried to include her in the conversation and how the King, remembering having seen her drinking beer on a previous occasion, had arranged for

Trophies of the Coronation that never was. A collection of glasses and goblets made in various European countries in anticipation of Edward's Coronation.

bottles of lager to be by her place at table. These are trivial details, admittedly, but remarkable at such a time. George VI recalled a dinner party on 8 December: "While the rest of us . . . were very sad (we knew of the final and irrevocable decision he had made) my brother was the life and soul of the party telling the P.M. things I am sure he had never heard before about unemployed centres etc (referring to his visit in S. Wales) I whispered to W.M. 'and this is the man we are going to lose'. One couldn't, nobody could, believe it." But two days later, Edward, "perfectly calm", was signing the Instrument of Abdication. And in the early morning of 12 December, as "H.M.S. *Fury* slid silently and unescorted out of Portsmouth Harbour", the long years of exile began.

In England the crisis was suddenly over. The anxieties which Mr Chamberlain had felt about the effect of the excitement on the Christmas trade were presumably calmed and the Stock Exchange greeted the departure of King Edward with a healthy spurt. The press began to congratulate the country on its new monarch. "Serious minded King George VI has many qualities to endear him to his people", proclaimed the *News Review*. "He is a better boxer than was Edward VIII, plays a stronger game of tennis—though he is left handed with the racket—enjoys grouse-shooting and has a mechanical bent." It needed Archbishop Lang's distasteful homily on Edward's "craving for private happiness" to provoke any reaction in favour of the former monarch.

Edward's adjustment to the position of Duke of Windsor was more difficult than that of England to King George VI. "By withdrawing from the great position which my birth had destined me to fill, I had become something alien, something apart." But he had always been that. What he was in fact discovering was that no role at all was worse even than one he did

September 1940. *Governor of the Bahamas.*

Moulin de la Tuillerie, Chevreuse Valley near Paris. This was the only house the Windsors actually owned. The Duchess once told Harold Nicolson, *We want to settle down and grow trees.*

One of the vast trunks that accompanied the Windsors on their travels.

not fit. The greatest infliction of his exile was not that of his reduced status (though he minded that for his wife); it was that he was bored and unoccupied. He was a man of considerable energy which was never again to find a worthwhile outlet. In his palmy days he had been hailed as "Britain's finest ambassador" and "Britain's best salesman". But now there was no opportunity to exercise these talents. Saddest of all was that, mingling exclusively with the rich and the worldly, he appeared to have banished even the memory of the man who had once shown compassionate regard for the unfashionable poor. It had been Mrs Simpson who had given him a taste for high society; now the Duchess of Windsor did not seem able to provide any other.

Probably he had hoped when he abdicated that he would soon return to England with the status of a younger brother of the King. This is what Chamberlain, who succeeded Baldwin as Prime Minister in 1937, wanted to accomplish. Lord Monckton, admittedly "*parti pris*" for Edward, judged that "The King himself, though he was not anxious for the Duke to return as early as November 1938 (which was what the Duke wanted) was not fundamentally against the Prime Minister's view. But I think the Queen felt quite plainly that it was undesirable to give the Duke any effective sphere of work. I felt then, as always, that she naturally thought that she must be on her guard because the Duke of Windsor, to whom the other brothers had always looked up, was an attractive, vital creature who might be the rallying point for any who might be critical of the new King who was less superficially endowed with the arts and graces that please." On the other hand, Edward also had himself to blame for his continued exclusion. He had an obstinate tendency to haggle over the conditions of his return, the most fatal example of which came in the summer of 1940.

He would have been an admirable salesman for Rolls-Royce but an ex-King cannot start selling motor cars. Duchess of Windsor to Harold Nicolson.

LEFT *The wife for whom the King gave up so great a heritage, and who has repaid his devotion with equal loyalty, companionship and love*, Lord Jellicoe speaking to the House of Lords, June 1972.

Towards the end of the Duke's life a visit from Princess Alexandra and Mr. Angus Ogilvy gave him great pleasure.

His memory will long survive as a story of high romance.

When Winston Churchill became Prime Minister he arranged for Edward, who had taken refuge in Spain after the collapse of France, to return immediately to Britain, even laying on flying boats for this purpose. But Edward adamantly refused to budge before receiving a guarantee that the royal family would receive his wife. To worry the Prime Minister about such matters at a time when Britain was bracing herself for invasion was worse than stupid. Had he returned then, an ex-king to his beleaguered former subjects, most likely his exile would have been over. As it was, after the fashion of Lord Lundy, he was sent out to govern the Bahamas, and an unique chance for conciliation was irrevocably lost.

The rest was trivia. There remained the soubriquet of Great Lover which the press bestowed on him and which not even their surfeit of saccharine could invalidate. The facts speak for themselves and cannot be gainsaid: they present a reputation which can only be judged corny because it is so obviously justified. But was this renown too extravagantly purchased? In 1938 Queen Mary set forth her views on the abdication in an admirably clear letter to Edward which will always remain the definitive statement of the orthodox royal reaction to his behaviour.

"You did not seem able to take in any point of view but your own . . . I do not think you have ever realised the shock, which the attitude you took up caused your family and the whole Nation. It seemed inconceivable to those who had made such sacrifices during the war that you, as their King, refused a lesser sacrifice . . ." All these points are unanswerable, but his mother's values are not the only ones by which Edward may be judged.

In leaving him it would be fairer to bear in mind Matthew Arnold's words about the fate of men of humanity: "They have,

RIGHT Homage to a King.

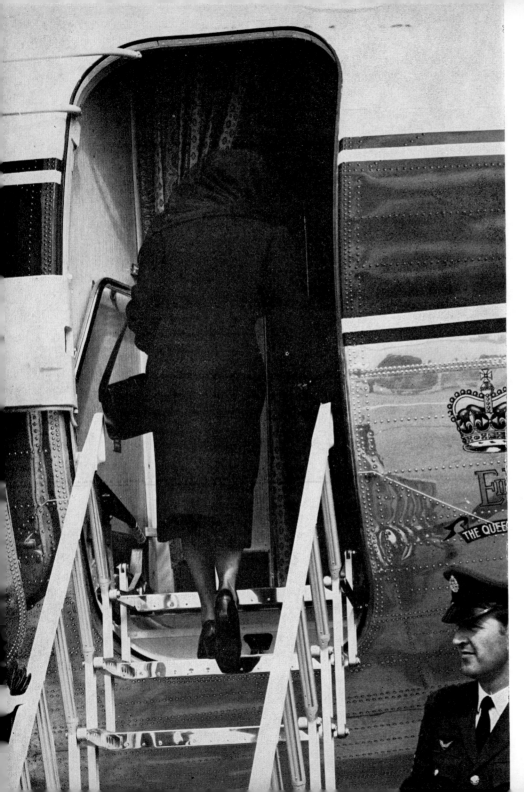

in general a rough time of it in their lives; but they are sewn more abundantly than one might think, they appear where and when one least expects it, they set up a fire which enfilades, so to speak the class with which they are ranked; ... and seasonably disconcert mankind in their worship of machinery".

The end of a love story. Alone the widowed Duchess leaves again for France.

THE HOROSCOPE OF THE DUKE OF WINDSOR

BORN: 23rd June, 1894   TIME: 10 p.m. GMT   PLACE: White Lodge, Richmond Park, Surrey

The Duke of Windsor was born when the Sun was in the Water-sign CANCER and the Moon, the 'ruler' of his sunsign, was itself in another Water-sign—PISCES. This means he had an extremely sensitive, affectionate, intuitive and idealistic nature. The prominence of the Moon in his horoscope, in the part connected with 'personality' gave him the 'common touch'—the ability to mix easily, a keen sympathy and understanding of people, and a tremendous zest for life, and the joys of life.

The rebel in his nature is indicated by the fact that when he was born AQUARIUS—the sign of the individualist—was on the Eastern horizon of his horoscope, and Uranus, the planet linked with Aquarius, was the most powerfully placed one in the whole horoscope, (incidentally Uranus is linked with divorce). These signs account for his strong non-conformist attitude, his challenge to the Establishment. Aquarius is also the sign of the humanitarian, the reformer. The fact that Aquarius was so strong in his chart, and also because the Sun was at a powerful angle to both Uranus and Mars, gave him the willpower to hold out against both Ministerial and family pressure at the time of the abdication.

The chart also clearly shows someone who would be torn between his sense of duty to the family (in this case the family being the nation as well as kindred) and his affections and love of personal freedom.

Other details of his life-history clearly reflected in his horoscope are as follows:—

His Abdication is shown by the position and aspects of the planet JUPITER at the time of his birth. Jupiter was the 'ruler' of his 10th house—his 'career' house; Jupiter was in the arc of the horoscope opposite this house, and closely linked there with the planets Neptune and Pluto. This would mean the 'throwing off' of status.

The Duke's marriage to a commoner who was of different nationality was indicated by the fact that the sun (the ruler of his 'marriage' house) was placed in his 5th house (love, romance) and in powerful aspect to the Moon in Pisces (the people) and both sun and moon were in powerful aspect to Uranus in the 9th house (connections abroad). Interpreted, this means a marriage, made for love, with a woman of the people who was also a foreigner.

Had Edward chosen to remain on the throne he would have been a very popular monarch, but financially the country would have suffered. World War II would still have taken place and we should still have had the break-up of Empire which has occurred. This is shown in the horoscope by Mars (planet of War) at a powerful but unfavourable angle to the Sun in Edward's horoscope; quite apart from the indication of War during his reign, it would also mean loss of overseas possessions through war or other causes.

KATINA THEODOSSIOU